Branch
Lines of
Oxfordshire

Branch Lines of Oxfordshire

Oxfordshire

COLIN G. MAGGS

ALAN SUTTON PUBLISHING LIMITED

First published in the United Kingdom in 1995
Alan Sutton Publishing Ltd · Phoenix Mill · Stroud · Gloucestershire

Copyright © Colin G. Maggs, 1995

British Library Cataloguing in Publication Data.

Maggs, Colin G.
Branch Lines of Oxfordshire
I. Title
385.094257

ISBN 0-7509-1024-0

Endpapers. Front: A 5101 class 2–6–2T, No. 5154, with the 4.53 p.m. Chipping Norton to Kingham train 1 mile north of Sarsden Halt. (31.8.62 Michael Mensing)
Back: Allan, a Peckett 0–6–0ST, working empty BR iron ore tippler wagons from the BR sidings to the quarry. Near Drayton, the engine is about to pass under the bridge carrying the A41. Right-hand running is being practised. (11.5.64 Michael Mensing)

Typesetting in 9/10 Palatino.
Typesetting and origination by
Alan Sutton Publishing Limited.
Printed and bound in Great Britain by
Butler & Tanner Ltd, Frome, Somerset.

Contents

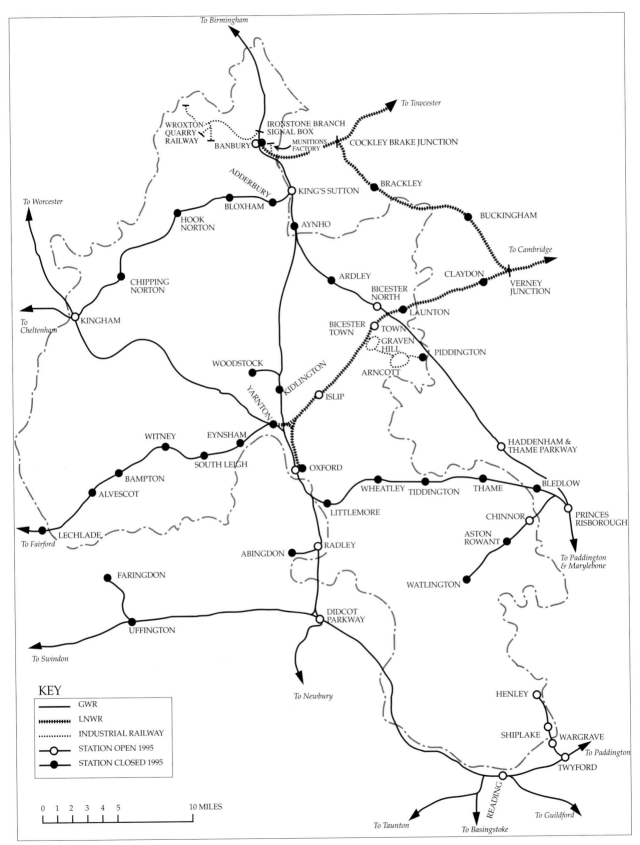

To Birmingham

To Towcester

WROXTON
QUARRY
RAILWAY

IRONSTONE BRANCH
SIGNAL BOX

MUNITIONS
FACTORY

COCKLEY BRAKE JUNCTION

BANBURY

ADDERBURY

KING'S SUTTON

BRACKLEY

To Worcester

BLOXHAM

AYNHO

BUCKINGHAM

HOOK
NORTON

To Cambridge

ARDLEY

CLAYDON

CHIPPING
NORTON

BICESTER
NORTH

LAUNTON

VERNEY
JUNCTION

To
Cheltenham

KINGHAM

BICESTER
TOWN

TOWN

GRAVEN
HILL

PIDDINGTON

WOODSTOCK

KIDLINGTON

ARNCOTT

YARNTON

ISLIP

WITNEY

EYNSHAM

HADDENHAM &
THAME PARKWAY

SOUTH LEIGH

OXFORD

BLEDLOW

BAMPTON

WHEATLEY

TIDDINGTON

THAME

ALVESCOT

LITTLEMORE

CHINNOR

PRINCES
RISBOROUGH

LECHLADE

ASTON
ROWANT

To Fairford

ABINGDON

RADLEY

To Paddington
& Marylebone

FARINGDON

WATLINGTON

UFFINGTON

DIDCOT
PARKWAY

To Swindon

HENLEY

To Newbury

SHIPLAKE

WARGRAVE

KEY

To Paddington

	GWR
	LNWR
	INDUSTRIAL RAILWAY
○	STATION OPEN 1995
●	STATION CLOSED 1995

TWYFORD

READING

0 1 2 3 4 5   10 MILES

To Taunton

To Basingstoke

To Guildford

BRANCH LINES OF OXFORDSHIRE

Introduction

The pattern of the railway map of Oxfordshire is based on the Great Western Railway (GWR) line from Paddington to Bristol, which was opened throughout in 1841. It skirted the southern boundary of the county, only briefly entering it in the environs of Goring. Didcot on this line was only 9½ miles from Oxford, so a branch was built to the city on 12 June 1844. The Oxford, Worcester & Wolverhampton Railway (OWWR) was an extension of this branch, and it rivalled the London & North Western Railway (LNWR) route to the Black Country. Originally intended to be a broad gauge line, the OWWR was opened on the standard gauge to Wolverton in April 1854 for goods and 1 July 1854 for passengers. Meanwhile the GWR had extended its Oxford branch as the broad gauge Birmingham & Oxford Railway, which opened to Banbury on 2 September 1850 and through to Birmingham on 1 October 1852. In due course the OWWR became part of the GWR and a few branches spread from these main lines.

The Oxford & Bletchley Junction Railway linked the LNWR's London to Birmingham line with Oxford and had the advantage that, in addition to serving the university town, it could link with the OWWR and siphon off traffic north of Oxford so that it went to Euston rather than Paddington. The OBJR reached Oxford on 20 May 1851.

The Buckinghamshire & Brackley Railway (BBR) amalgamated with the OBJR to become the Buckinghamshire Railway. This line, associated with the LNWR, opened to Banbury on 1 May 1850. From 1 June 1872 another of the LNWR's allies, the Northampton & Banbury Junction Railway (NBJR), reached Banbury over Buckinghamshire Railway metals.

One GWR main line was still to be built. At the turn of the century critics of the GWR claimed that the company's initials stood for 'Great Way Round', and certainly quite a few of its main routes were not beelines. This criticism applied to the GWR's route between Paddington and Birmingham via Oxford. A route 19 miles shorter was planned using existing and new track between Old Oak Common Junction and Aynho Junction, which opened in 1910. Expresses were withdrawn from this line in 1968 and some of the line was singled. It then had branch line, rather than main line, status.

Most of the Oxfordshire branches were closed either completely or partly in the 1950s and '60s. The Oxford to Princes Risborough line lost its central section, but the ends continued to be used, while the Watlington line remained open as a 'long siding' to Chinnor. The Oxford to Bletchley line lost its passenger services, but these have since been reinstated between Bicester Town and Oxford.

In this volume, branches are described starting at Henley and proceeding in an anticlockwise direction round the county as it was before the 1974 boundary revision.

Grateful thanks are due to E.J.M. Hayward for checking and improving the text and captions.

GREAT WESTERN RAILWAY.

(For the use of the Company's Servants only.)

NOTICE OF

SPECIAL TRAIN

FROM

WINDSOR

TO

BLENHEIM

AND BACK,

ON

Friday, November 24th, 1899.

TIME TABLE.

FORWARD JOURNEY.		pass arr. P.M.	pass dep. NOON	RETURN JOURNEY.		pass arr. P.M.	pass dep. P.M.
WINDSOR		—	12 0	BLENHEIM			
Slough West Curve	**A**	ML 12 6		Kidlington			
Maidenhead			12 12	Oxford (Middle Road)			
Reading			12 24	Didcot East Junction			
Didcot East Junction			12 43	Reading			
Oxford (Middle Road)			12 56	Maidenhead			
Kidlington ...	**B**	1 4	1 7	Slough West Curve ...			
BLENHEIM		1 15	—	WINDSOR			

Time of return uncertain.

Special will probably leave **Blenheim about 3.30 p.m.**

Station Masters at all Stations must be on the look out for telegraphic advice and must endeavour to keep a clear road for the Special.

A To precede the 11.45 a.m. Express from Paddington from Slough.

B A Separate Engine to be provided at Kidlington on Down journey to enable Train Engine to be detached there and run to Oxford to turn. Train Engine to return to Blenheim in good time to work the Special Train through from there to Windsor.

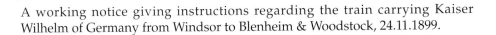

A working notice giving instructions regarding the train carrying Kaiser Wilhelm of Germany from Windsor to Blenheim & Woodstock, 24.11.1899.

Wargrave to Henley-on-Thames

A bill for building a branch from Twyford to Henley was put forward unsuccessfully in 1846. A second attempt made the following year led to an Act being passed on 22 July 1847, but the depression that set in following the Railway Mania (1844–7) delayed construction. No positive action was taken until powers were revived by an Act of 4 August 1853, Messrs A.W. Ritson beginning construction during the winter of 1854/5. Work was easy, except for Shiplake Viaduct, a 230 yd long timber bridge, across the Thames into Oxfordshire. This structure was subject to a 20 m.p.h. speed limit.

The single, broad gauge line opened on 1 June 1857, the first train being hauled by 'Leo' class 2–4–0T *Virgo*. A public breakfast was held at Henley Town Hall. The five trains each way connected at Twyford with Up rather than Down trains, so were not convenient for passengers travelling west. As no reduced fares were available from Henley, some passengers bound for London travelled to Reading by road coach in order to avail themselves of cheap tickets. The opening of the branch rendered redundant the four-horse coach that ran twice daily between Henley and Twyford.

The line was converted to standard gauge in 1876, the penultimate solely broad gauge branch east of Bristol to be changed. Work started at 9.30 p.m. on 31 March and was completed in 12 hours. A civil engineer, R.M. Parkinson, recollected his experiences of the task in the *Great Western Railway Magazine* of December 1941:

I found myself at nine o'clock one evening in the company of two permanent-way inspectors in a packer's hut midway between Twyford and Henley. The slopes of the railway were covered with men, but all one could hear was the distant sound of an engine shunting in Henley station yard. At length there came a whistle and we could hear the approaching train, followed by a kind of roar which developed into, 'Now, all together, over,' with a grunt like a miner's, when he brings his sledge down on the drill.

Directly the train had passed, every one was alive. Each inspector had four gangs of five and twenty men in his mile. Two of the twenty-five went ahead knocking out the fastening, two pairs followed cutting the transoms which had already been marked, and two more followed the main gang refixing the bolts and straps. By midnight the line on our two miles had been slewed in from 7 ft. 0¼ in. to the 4 ft. 8½ in. gauge, and we retired to our hut to feed and, as we hoped, to sleep. But not so; one of the inspectors, being of the opinion that if we did not keep awake we should catch cold, threw a fog signal into the fire and we promptly moved out. I then walked towards Twyford, where progress had been slower, as the line was curved and the rails had to be cut in many places. At 4 a.m. we were about again, but there was not sufficient light for an hour to lift and pack the rails, though we managed to get a train through by eight o'clock.

Henley developed as a popular holiday resort and dormitory town, and business during the summer was often brisk. To cope with this traffic, in 1897 the track was doubled and the junction at Twyford improved to give through-running to and from Paddington. It was also planned to extend the Bourne End to Marlow branch to link with the existing line at Henley, but this scheme would have disturbed the peace of the river, and was successfully opposed by rowing clubs.

The branch helped Henley Regatta to become more popular as it facilitated access. In 1898, 37,513 passengers were carried over the three days. In 1902, twenty-seven special trains were run from Paddington to Henley each day, twelve of these running non-stop. Additionally there were through trains from Didcot, Oxford and Windsor. Extra staff, who were needed to cope with the traffic, were drafted in from as far away as Bradford-on-Avon, Chester, Hereford, Liskeard and Wrexham. As lodgings were difficult to find at this busy period, the GWR stabled a dining saloon and coach at Henley to accommodate these extra staff. The number of passengers carried to the regatta declined from 1906, and by 1953 only three special trains were run.

The branch pioneered Automatic Train Control when, in January 1906, audible distant signals were introduced. The apparatus consisted of a ramp formed by an insulated steel bar on a baulk of timber laid centrally between the rails and a spring contact shoe under the engine, so fixed as to be raised by 1½ inches when passing over the ramp. If the distant signal was at 'All Clear', the ramp was electrified and the current passing through the shoe rang a bell in the engine cab; but if the signal was at 'Caution', or any failure occurred, the ramp remained electrically dead and the raising of the shoe broke a local circuit on the engine, thereby causing a steam whistle to blow in the cab until silenced by the driver.

During the Second World War, ambulance trains headed by London & North Eastern Railway (LNER) B12 class 4–6–0s worked to Henley, carrying wounded to the hospital at Kingswood Common.

As an economy measure the branch was singled on 16 June 1961, and from 20 March 1972 Reading panel-box controlled the branch. The *GWR Service Timetable Appendices* for 1945 stated that signal lamps on the branch must not be lit from 1 April until 30 September.

The southern half of the Henley branch is in Berkshire, but it enters Oxfordshire as it crosses the Thames Viaduct over the river. This consists of eleven spans of wrought iron plate girders resting on blue brick and cast iron piers. It is followed by Lashbrook Viaduct, which has six spans, totals 93 yd and is of similar construction to the Thames Viaduct.

Not far beyond Lashbrook Viaduct is Shiplake station. Originally a timber building, it was destroyed by fire on 26 August 1891. The following year it was replaced by a red brick construction. When the line was doubled in 1898 the platform was made into an island. In 1913 the station was converted from oil lighting to the rare petrol-air-gas system: the gas was collected over a water tank, and bunsen burners were used in winter to prevent the water from freezing. This form of lighting proved unsatisfactory and was replaced by electricity. A replacement signal-box was opened on 14 June 1961. It was of prefabricated construction and had a natural timber finish. Although modern in style, its dull design quickly dated. At one time a camp coach was stationed at Shiplake.

The station closed to goods on 7 September 1964. Today only the Up side of the platform is used. It has been made most attractive by planting numerous beds of shrubs along its centre. A sizeable free car park is adjacent. Apart from its use by commuters, the train is taken by Shiplake people going to Henley to shop, thus avoiding traffic and parking problems.

Immediately north of the station is a level-crossing protected by lights. Normally clear

HENLEY BRANCH.

Passengers between London and the Henley Branch will have to change Carriages at Twyford.

DOWN.

Distance				Week Days									Sundays				
			1 & 2 class.	1, 2, 3 class.	1 & 2 class.	1 & 2 class.		1 & 2 class.	1 & 2 class.	1, 2, 3 class.		1, 2, 3 class.			1 & 2 class.	1 & 2 class.	1 & 2 class.
			a.m.	a.m.	a.m.	p.m.		p.m.	p.m.	p.m.		a.m.			p.m.	p.m.	p.m.
—	London	Paddington Stn. Dep.	.	7 5	10 0	12 20	.	3 40	5 10	7 0	.	9 0	.	.	2 30	4 45	7 0
		Victoria ,,	..	..	8 55	11 47	..	..	..	6 32	..	8 35	..	..	1 35	4 0	6 10
		Kensington ,,	...	...	9 15	12 10	...	...	...	6 52	..	8 54	...	...	1 54	4 20	6 30
31	TWYFORD Arr.		..	8 23	11 5	1 48	..	4 20	6 20	8 23	..	10 18	..	..	3 42	5 58	8 23
	Dep.		7 30	8 50	11 10	1 53	...	4 27	6 25	8 27	...	10 23	...	...	3 47	6 3	8 27
34	SHIPLAKE		7 40	9 0	11 20	2 3	..	4 37	6 35	8 37	..	10 33	.	.	3 57	6 13	8 37
35½	Henley Arr.		7 45	9 5	11 25	2 8	..	4 42	6 40	8 42	..	10 38	..	..	4 2	6 18	8 42

UP.

Dist.			Week Days								Sundays					
			1, 2, 3 class.	1 & 2 class.	1 & 2 class.		1 & 2 class.	1, 2, 3 class.	1, 2, 3 class.	1 & 2 class.		1 & 2 class.		1,2,3 class.	1, 2, 3 class.	1 & 2 class.
			a.m.	a.m.	a.m.		p.m.	p.m.	p.m.	p.m.		a.m.		p.m.	p.m.	p.m.
—	Henley	Dep.	7 5	8 30	10 45	.	1 5	3 35	5 55	8 0	.	9 0	.	1 45	5 35	7 55	.
1¾	SHIPLAKE		7 10	8 34	10 50	.	1 10	3 39	6 0	8 5	..	9 5	..	1 50	5 40	8 0	..
4¾	TWYFORD Arr.		7 20	8 44	11 0	..	1 20	3 48	6 10	8 15	...	9 15	...	1 58	5 50	8 10	...
	Dep.		7 27	8 47	11 7	...	1 35	4 17	6 22	8 22	..	9 25	..	2 0	5 57	8 12	...
	London	Kensington Station Arr.	9 5	10 16	12 37	..	.	5 45	7 37	..	..	..	..	3 22	7 40	..	..
		Victoria ,,	9 23	10 35	12 55	..	..	5 2	7 55	...	...	...	...	3 40	7 58	...	...
35½		Paddington ,,	8 55	9 40	12 35	...	2 40	5 45	7 35	9 55	..	10 45	..	3 15	7 35	9 40	..

The timetable for June 1865.

to road vehicles, an approaching train works a treadle to trigger the red lights for road traffic. A Down train stops at the platform immediately before the treadle and so does not operate it until it starts to move. This prevents road traffic from being delayed unnecessarily.

The train shed at Henley covered the concourse and 100 ft of platforms. The Up and Down platforms were each double-sided, the centre road serving both. A 200 ft long canopy was added to the Up platform in 1904. The original columns of the train shed were sawn off 2 to 3 ft above ground level and replaced by broad gauge bridge rail. A brick building in front of the terminal end of the station was erected in about 1900. On 1 January 1895 'on Thames' was added to the station's name to avoid confusion with Henley-in-Arden, which had been opened the previous year. No. 1 platform, the westernmost, was taken out of use in 1969 and No. 3 platform was renumbered No. 1. In 1984 a joint scheme between the British Rail (BR) Property Board and Hallmark Cards Ltd redeveloped the station. This involved the demolition of the old station and the building of a new one, with an adjacent three-storey office block for Hallmark on the site of the train shed. This entailed shortening the branch by about 200 feet. Passenger facilities in the new single-road station, also brick-built, include a ticket office, a café and a large car park. The goods shed, situated on the west side of the passenger station, was in Gothic style, and built of brick and stone.

Henley closed to goods traffic on 7 September 1964 and the coal siding was lifted in 1969. Seven long sidings were provided for storing coaches, and these were particularly useful during regatta week. In the immediate post-war years these sidings were full of coaches awaiting renovation after years of wartime neglect. Latterly they housed vehicles that were used only for peak holiday workings.

The two types of passenger train at Henley utilized different locomotives: direct trains to Paddington used engines of the 'Hall' and 'Castle' classes, whereas the shuttle service to Reading was worked by steam railmotor, and later by an 0–4–2T and auto-coaches.

At the turn of the century, 517 class 0–4–2Ts and 'Metro' class 2–4–0Ts worked the branch, staying until the early 1930s. On 4 May 1914 they were joined by steam railmotors. During the 1930s, 57XX 0–6–0PTs were allocated to Henley shed. At the end of the Second World War the 57XX class took sole control of local services until the 94XX 0–6–0PTs shared these duties. From February 1934, GWR diesel railcars appeared on some workings. In 1937 they were replaced by 48XX class 0–4–2T and auto-coach, which travelled 240 miles daily – one of the hardest auto turns in the country.

Although through services to Paddington were sometimes in charge of a 'Metro', generally these trains were worked by tender engines, such as 0–6–0s of the Standard Goods and Dean Goods varieties; 'Barnum' class 2–4–0s; 'Duke', 'Atbara', 'Bulldog', 'City', 'Flower' and 'County' class 4–4–0s; 43XX 2–6–0s; 'Hall', 'Castle' and 'Saint' 4–6–0s; and even a BR Standard 'Britannia' class Pacific.

A single-road, brick-built engine was provided at Henley. The non-standard water-tower built by the contractor incorporated a coaling stage, but this was out of use by 1897, locomotives then being coaled directly from a wagon to avoid the double transhipment of this heavy commodity. In about 1904 the arches of the water-tower were boarded to create a cabin for the overnight shedman to sleep in. It later became the cleaners' store. Steam to power the water pump came from the low sounding whistle of a locomotive, and although an electric pump was installed in 1950, steam remained as a standby. On regatta days an engine stood by ready to provide steam for the water pump as a large quantity of water was required by visiting engines. In 1903 the 45 ft diameter turntable was replaced by one of 55 ft at a cost of £2,800. A tender had to be full to balance an engine on this table. It was so little used that it required several men to turn an engine, and 'several men' were available on regatta days.

The last steam-hauled branch train to Henley ran on Sunday 5 October 1958, and the following day a single unit Diesel Multiple Unit (DMU) began, but through trains to and from Paddington and the branch goods trains continued to be steam-hauled. The last steam through trains ran on 14 June 1963.

In 1857, six trains ran each way taking 15 minutes for the distance of 4½ miles from Twyford to Henley. By 1887 the service had improved to eleven Down, twelve Up and six each way on Sundays, taking 10–12 minutes. The daily service in 1910 was twenty-one each way and seven on Sundays. By 1922 the numbers were thirty-four Down and thirty Up, and on Sundays fourteen and fifteen respectively. Today there are twenty-four Down and twenty-three Up workings, and twelve each way on Sundays. On weekdays the 07.35 ex-Henley runs through to Paddington and the 17.53 from Paddington through to Henley. In the middle of the day and late evenings, trains run through to and from Reading. All Saturday trains are to and from Reading, while all Sunday trains shuttle between Twyford and Henley.

From the summer of 1902, combined rail and river excursions were run to Henley. During the early 1900s, in June and July, a through service ran on Sundays from Victoria to Henley, setting down at Taplow, Maidenhead, Wargrave and Shiplake. The train was usually hauled by a 'Metro' class 2–4–0T.

In July 1911 the passenger train formation was two compos and two brake thirds. Following the Second World War the branch was worked by two pairs of ex-slip coaches, the pairs usually alternating each week. Today the branch is worked by Class 165/1 Network Turbos.

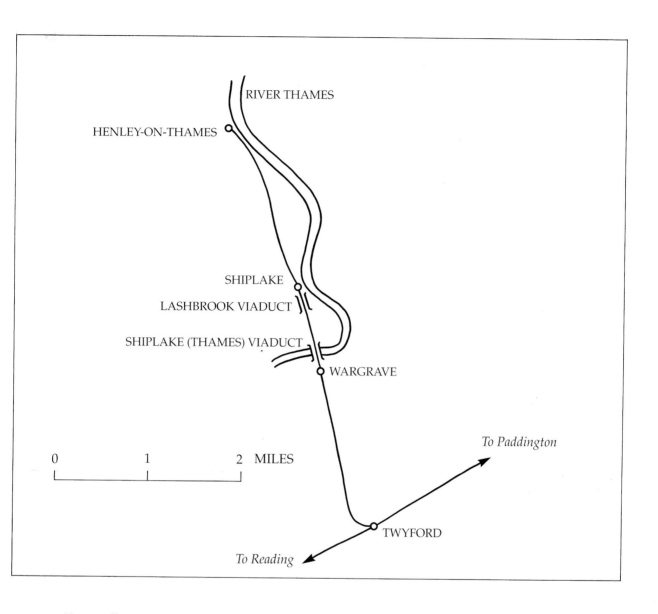

RIVER THAMES

HENLEY-ON-THAMES

SHIPLAKE

LASHBROOK VIADUCT

SHIPLAKE (THAMES) VIADUCT

WARGRAVE

To Paddington

0   1   2   MILES

TWYFORD

To Reading

Key to all maps:

——————	Great Western Railway
++++++++++	London & North Western Railway
··············	Industrial Railway
—O—	Station open 1995
—●—	Station closed 1995

Timber viaduct over the River Thames.
c. 1895 Author's collection

'Metro' class 2–4–0T No. 463 at Shiplake with a Down train on the new track, which was laid in 1898. The fireman is looking back to watch for the guard's 'Right Away'. An Up train stands at the other platform. Notice the canopy all round the station building.

c. 1905 Lens of Sutton

Shiplake, view Up. The rail in the sidings is laid on longitudinal sleepers. The yard crane was for lifting goods on or off wagons. The footbridge gave access to the platform and also allowed pedestrians to cross when the level-crossing gates were closed across the road.

c. 1905 Author's collection

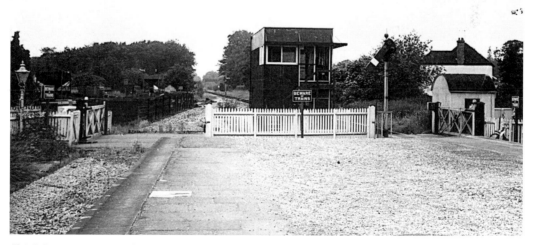

Shiplake, view Down, showing the new signal-box, which was opened on 14 June 1961. On the left is the trackbed of the Down loop, which was lifted on 15 June 1969. The footbridge has been removed.

23.6.71 D. Payne

The GWR-style station nameboard in the car park.

6.5.95 Author

Rear view of Class 165/1 Network Turbo 165135 with the 09.42 Saturdays-only Reading to Henley service.

6.5.95 Author

A treadle depressed by wheel flanges for working the lights at Shiplake level-crossing.

6.5.95 Author

Crowds arriving at Henley for the regatta.

c. 1905 Lens of Sutton

The exterior of Henley station. The new booking hall was added to the front of the train shed in 1903. The roof of the latter can be seen on the far right.

c. 1910 Author's collection

The impressive large signal-box at Henley. The GWR frame contained sixty-five levers, but this was replaced in 1956 with one of fifty-four levers. An electric panel was installed in 1961. The box closed on 20 March 1972.

23.6.71 D. Payne

This 94XX class 0–6–0PT, No. 9403, is apparently awaiting departure from Henley. It was not unusual for the Henley branch trains to carry the headcode shown. On the left are two converted slip-coaches.

c. 1953 Lens of Sutton

Class 165/1 Network Turbo 165135 at Henley station with the 11.06 Saturdays-only train to Reading. Beyond the platform canopy is the Hallmark Card building on the site of the former train shed. The station offices protrude to the left beyond the canopy, while on the far left can be seen part of the large car park, most of which is on the site of the former goods yard.

6.5.95 Author

Wainhill Crossing Halt to Watlington

The Wallingford & Watlington Railway Act was passed on 27 July 1864, but only the section from Cholsey and Moulsford to Wallingford was constructed.

The Watlington & Princes Risborough Railway (W&PRR) Act of 26 July 1869 was promoted largely by the Earl of Macclesfield of Shirburn Castle, near Watlington. The Act authorized a capital of £36,000. To minimize earthworks the branch line chiefly followed the lie of the land and so had a switchback nature. For additional economy, chalk ballast was used. The company's first manager was J.G. Rowe, who was also secretary of the Aylesbury & Buckingham Railway.

The line opened on 15 August 1872 but, owing to a dispute with the GWR, at Princes Risborough through passengers had to alight at a small wooden platform and walk to the GWR station. A through connection was provided for the interchange of goods traffic. Single fares were first class 2s 3d; second class 1s 6d, third class 1s 1d and parliamentary class 9d. They altered little through the years, and in 1956 the single fare from Kingston Crossing Halt to Aston Rowant was only 2d.

Traffic was light and the directors kept services running at their own expense. At first locomotives were hired from the GWR and in 1875 a special undertaking, the Watlington Rolling Stock Company, was formed to supply the line with locomotives and coaches. By October 1876 the company owed the GWR £2,000, and that same year an agreement was signed, which allowed the W&PRR to use the junction and GWR station at Princes Risborough for the five years ending 31 December 1881 for £250 annually.

Finances improved in 1877 and the company was able to pay 3 per cent interest on the cash advanced by the directors. That year the GWR refused to work the line, saying that its light construction would require special locomotives, so those of the Watlington Rolling Stock Company continued in use.

A special meeting was held on 16 June 1883 to consider the GWR's offer of £23,000 for a line that had cost £46,522. At a further meeting, held the following month, these terms were accepted, and the GWR took possession on 31 December 1883. The value of the rolling-stock from the Watlington Rolling Stock Company was estimated to be £1,714. Its two tank engines were taken over by the GWR, one eventually being sold to the Weston, Clevedon & Portishead Light Railway in 1903.

Thomas Taylor, chairman of the W&PRR and rather an odd character, failed to transfer plans and sections of the line to Paddington, and attempts to obtain them were met with evasive replies. No proper conveyances of land had been drawn up when the company was first constituted. The GWR withheld payment of minor sums until the documents and plans were produced. One day, Taylor arrived at Watlington station with workmen to remove various stores and scrap metal, which he claimed were his. Resolving the

Chinnor, view Down. The platform side of the station building has been cement-rendered.

12.5.56 E. Wilmshurst

problem was the subject of considerable correspondence between Taylor and Sir Daniel Gooch, chairman of the GWR.

On 18 August 1883 the GWR directors authorized the expenditure of £3,750 to improve the branch. One rectification was to the fencing, though this failed to satisfy the wishes of a farmer at Lewknor, who desired the company to build a fence sufficiently high to prevent his turkeys from flying over it.

On 1 May 1890 the GWR obtained Board of Trade sanction to cancel the undertaking given by the W&PRR to work the line on the staff and ticket system – the GWR thus avoided the expense of installing the block telegraph. On 1 September 1906, steam railmotors were introduced and rail level halts opened at Bledlow Bridge, Kingston Crossing and Lewknor Bridge. When the railmotors ceased, an auto-coach was used as this, like the railmotors, had retractable steps to enable passengers to entrain at low-level platforms. It also enabled the guard to issue tickets to passengers boarding at such halts. Wainhill Crossing Halt opened in September 1925.

The branch closed to passengers on 1 July 1957, the last train running on 29 June. Chinnor to Watlington closed to freight on 2 January 1961, the final train running on 30 December 1960, and hauled by London Midland Region Class 2 2-6-2T No. 41272. Following the closure of Chinnor to goods traffic on 10 October 1966, the branch operated as a 'long siding', the guard obtaining from the Princes Risborough signalman the key to unlock the ground frames at Chinnor. The key was that formerly used on the Denham East to Uxbridge High Street branch and was so stamped.

The first station in Oxfordshire on the branch was Wainhill Crossing Halt and, like all of the other halts on this branch, consisted of a rail-level platform and timber waiting hut. Beyond, the line rises at 1 in 73/88 for ¾ mile, descending just before Chinnor. This was the principal intermediate station and was sited on the Up side of the track. An attractive, twin-pavilion design, it was constructed with red brick and flint walls. Its lintels were of Gothic style, it had pleasingly shaped bargeboards and decorative ridge tiles. Space was provided for a passing loop, should this have proved necessary. The station garden was well tended. For the benefit of goods engines shunting the two sidings, a water tank wagon was provided. Chinnor closed to goods on 10 October 1966, the goods shed having been removed before 1921.

Chinnor lime works was established in 1908 by William Elijah Benton and also produced cement from 1919. The raw material, chalk, was quarried locally. Around 240 tons of cement were produced weekly, and by 1928 improved equipment enabled production to be raised to 500 tons. The Chinnor Cement & Lime Co. Ltd was formed in 1936. By 1958, weekly capacity had been risen to 4,500 tons per week. The 1989 output was 5,600 tons. On 1 January 1963 the Chinnor Industries Group was acquired by the Rugby Portland Cement Co. Ltd.

Monthly tonnage of incoming coal and outgoing cement from Chinnor:

Period	Coal (tons per month)	Gypsum (tons per month)
1908–19	100	0 (only lime made)
1919–27	300	100
1927–34	1,000	200
1934–6	1,300	300
1936–56	2,700	650
1956–68	5,200	1,300

In 1968 the works' monthly requirements were about 400 wagons of coal and 100 wagons of gypsum from Kegworth in Nottinghamshire. Until 1928 all cement and lime was despatched by rail. From 1928 until 1940 about half was sent by rail and in 1968 only 130 tons (six Presflo wagons) was sent away by rail monthly (to Redland Pipes, Parkstone). Most of the cement was despatched to other destinations by road.

At the works, coal wagons were run individually by gravitation to the tippler and, after emptying, rolled by gravity to sidings to await collection. At a later date, hopper wagons were used. In 1979 a Class 31 from Old Oak Common worked the 07.46 to Chinnor. At High Wycombe, a driver and guard who were based there took over the train, and they were joined in due course by the Princes Risborough shunter. A twenty-wagon limit was imposed on a Down trip as the run-round loop at Chinnor only held this number. If the train was longer it had to be divided at Princes Risborough. Between Princes Risborough and Chinnor, trains were allowed 18 minutes Down and 15 minutes Up. Loaded trains approached Wainhill Crossing on a rising gradient of 1 in 73, so to avoid problems restarting, a crew member raced to open the gates before the train stopped. If it slipped severely the crew either placed sand on the rail by hand, or divided the train and returned for the second portion.

In 1989 the hopper wagons used for carrying the coal to Chinnor were declared obsolete by BR. Compared with the cost of road transport, their replacement was uneconomic. Class 47 No. 47258 and thirty-five hopper wagons made the final journey on 20 December 1989, the locomotive bearing a headboard that read: 'Last BR Train on the Watlington Branch'.

The line undulated to Kingston Crossing Halt, protected by distant signals (the only working signals on the branch) which were operated from a small frame and interlocked with the gates. Unusually for the GWR, these signals were on lattice posts.

Aston Rowant, like Chinnor, had provision for a Down loop line. The station building was similar to that at Chinnor and the initial track layout was a mirror image of Chinnor's. In 1950, scenes for the film *Portrait of Clare* were shot at the station. It closed to goods on 2 January 1961. Lewknor Bridge Halt opened on 1 September 1906.

Watlington station was similar in architecture to Aston Rowant and Chinnor. It had a short platform of only about two coaches in length, but by the late 1920s a slightly raised timber extension had been added at the buffer stops end to cater for milk traffic. At the other end of the platform was a cattle pen. Electric lighting was installed in 1936. During the Second World War a corrugated asbestos cycle shelter was erected on the site of the station garden. Prior to the 1880s a functional, rather than aesthetically pleasing, corrugated iron shelter was built opposite the platform for the branch coaches, in latter days an autotrailer. This was cleaned on Sunday mornings, with step ladders and planking being used for the more inaccessible areas.

The three sidings in the goods yard were worked from a ground frame that had been the signal-box until 1929. The goods shed was constructed of timber on a brick and flint base. No yard crane was provided, a travelling crane being sent from Reading when it was required.

The engine used for hauling the first trains was probably hired from the GWR. W&PRR No. 1 was a Sharp Stewart 2–2–2WT, believed to have been built in 1857 and run as Furness Railway No. 11 until 1873. No. 2 was a 2–4–0T from the same builder. No. 1 was scrapped in 1883 when the GWR took over, but No. 2, which dated from 1876, was rebuilt as GWR No. 1384. From 1886 it worked on several GWR branches before being withdrawn in 1911, when it was sold to the Weston, Clevedon & Portishead Light Railway, where it became No. 4 *Hesperus*. It was finally cut up in June 1937.

In about 1900 the branch was worked by 2–4–0T and 0–4–2T locomotives, while 2021 class 0–6–0ST/PTs were used for goods trains from the early 1900s until 1951. No. 2112 was on the branch from 1930 until 1951, when the 57XX and 74XX classes took over, with 850 class 0–6–0PTs making rare appearances. Occasionally a 14XX class 0–4–2T was used, but this was less successful hauling goods trains.

Following the arrival of the 8.40 a.m. at Princes Risborough each Monday morning, the branch locomotive was changed for a 'new' engine, which carried a week's supply of firelighters and cotton waste. It usually faced Watlington to ensure that the firebox crown was not uncovered, thereby causing the fusible plug to melt when tackling Chinnor bank. The branch engine ceased to be stabled at Watlington from about 1954, when the regular fireman was called up for National Service and no replacement could be found. In February 1955 a J68 class 0–6–0T from Aylesbury shed was tried over the line, but it lacked sufficient water capacity. In 1956 the branch engine departed from Slough at 5.38 a.m., arriving at Watlington, 33 miles distant, at 7.00 a.m. It returned after the last service, departing from Watlington at 9.00 p.m. and arriving at Slough by 10.50 p.m.

In 1968, North British Type 2 diesel-hydraulic D63XX class worked trains to and from Chinnor and also to Thame.

The timber-built locomotive shed at Watlington was burned down in September 1906, scorching the 0–6–0PT and 2–4–0T inside. It was never replaced, engines being kept over the pit. The 'shed' closed in June 1957.

At Watlington in 1937 there were two drivers and three firemen supplying crew for the two turns, plus a fireman for night duties such as cleaning, oiling, coaling, engine preparation and pumping water to the conical tank. Two electric pumps were installed in

November 1935, but the steam equipment was retained for use when the electricity supply, or the electric pumps, failed. The steam pumps were worked by two pipes: one from the train heating pipe to raise water to ground level; one, replacing the whistle, to feed the locomotive supply tank.

Firemen worked the night shift in rotation. As there was no engine shed, all their work had to be done in the open. A grounded horsebox at the end of the locomotive siding served as a loco stores and mess room until it was burned down in 1951, when some overalls that were being dried caught light. Its replacement was a timber-built hut that combined the loco mess with a permanent way men's hut but, in practice, loco men used a brake van permanently stabled in the cattle dock siding.

Relief men were provided by Slough shed, and they lodged at the public house. Saturday relief work for an unsuspecting Slough fireman meant fire-dropping at Watlington at 8.30 p.m., then cycling on the Watlington station bicycle to Princes Risborough to catch the 8.30 a.m. Sunday train back to Slough.

Times varied slightly throughout the years that engines were stabled at Watlington, but the day started by working the 5.50 a.m. goods, or engine and brake van, to Princes Risborough. Having collected wagons for the branch, the loco reached Watlington at 8.18 a.m. A note in the working timetable ordered: 'Important this Goods trip works to time to enable the 8.40 a.m. passenger from Watlington to start punctually'. At Watlington the wagons had to be shunted into a siding, the auto-coach collected from its carriage shed and the engine tanks topped up with water. The 8.40 a.m. passenger train, in addition to calling at all stations and halts, stopped when required at Shirburn Farm occupation crossing about ¾ mile from the terminus. The 3.55 p.m. from Princes Risborough also stopped at this crossing if required.

Daily average of wagons dealt with on the Watlington branch, 1925:

Coal & mineral		General goods		No. of milk cans	No. of livestock trucks
Forward	Received	Forward	Received	per annum	per annum
6	17	15	8	29,087	150

Traffic: lime, cement, farm products

The single-line branch was worked by a train staff and one engine in steam, or two coupled together. The staff, round in shape and coloured black, had a key on its end to unlock points at intermediate stations' ground frames. As the line was technically a light railway, speed was restricted to 30 m.p.h. Latterly, when operated as a 'long siding', speed was limited to 20 m.p.h. Whistle boards – a black 'W' on a white background – warned a driver when he was approaching the most used occupation crossings.

The initial passenger service of three each way on weekdays only had by 1875 become five each way and two on Sundays, the time taken for the 9 miles being 30 minutes. By 1887 there were only three trains on weekdays, taking 35 minutes. By 1910 this number had risen to six and in 1922 the five trains were allowed 25 minutes for the journey. Good connections at Princes Risborough gave a time of just over 1 hour from Watlington to Paddington. There was considerable milk traffic and a fair quantity of freight, two goods trains running daily plus one from Princes Risborough to Chinnor and back. In the 1930s an occasional excursion train consisting of three or four coaches of ramblers bound for the Roman Ridgeway ran on a Sunday. In 1956, five Up and four Down passenger trains were run and an extra round-trip was made at midday on Saturdays. The timetable was unbalanced as the first train from Watlington returned empty stock. The last Down passenger train made a connection with the slip-coach off the 7.10 p.m. Paddington to Birmingham.

The last BR train to Chinnor, on 20 December 1989, did not signal the end of trains on the branch. The Chinnor & Princes Risborough Railway (CPRR) Association, which was formed in August 1989, took over the line's maintenance from 20 December 1989. In May 1994 it erected a new, authentic-looking platform at Chinnor, almost on the site of the original. A Cambrian Railways grounded coach body serves as a waiting-room, booking office and sales area. Wainhill Crossing Halt has been restored but cannot be opened to traffic because of a lack of parking facilities for passengers – even turning a vehicle is almost impossible.

In August 1994 the CPRR Association purchased the freehold of the branch, and on the 20th of that month it operated round trips from Chinnor to Wainhill Crossing Halt and back. The following April, passenger services were extended to Thame Junction, where a run-round loop had been constructed. A connection to the Chiltern line at Princes Risborough has been maintained, and it is hoped that access agreements will eventually allow the branch train to use the Watlington bay platform once more.

The CPRR Association has restored Bledlow Bridge Halt, though this too has not been opened to the public because of parking problems. Other buildings owned by the association are Gerrards Cross signal-box, which is currently in storage, as is the lever frame from Bradford Junction, Wiltshire. The association looks after Princes Risborough signal-box, a Grade II listed building. It has 124 levers, only seven fewer than Exeter West, Britain's largest preserved signal-box, which has been restored and rests at the Crewe Heritage Centre. The association has plans to rebuild Chinnor station, erect locomotive and carriage sheds at Princes Risborough, and reopen the line between Chinnor and Aston Rowant.

CPRR stock list:

Class 08 0–6–0 diesel-electric *Haversham* was originally No. 13018 and delivered new in 1953 to Willesden shed. In July 1958 it became D3018, then in June 1974 it became No. 08011. The oldest working diesel on BR, it was painted in its original green livery and named *Haversham* by the staff at Bletchley. As it had no air brakes, BR withdrew it from traffic on 16 December 1991 and it was purchased by the association on 25 April 1992.

D8568 Bo-Bo diesel-electric, built by the Clayton Equipment Co. in January 1964, is the only member of the 117-strong class still extant. First allocated to Haymarket shed, Edinburgh, it was sold for industrial use in 1972, eventually arriving at Chinnor on 25 April 1992.

Ruston & Hornsby Ltd 0–6–0 diesel-hydraulic, works No. 459515, was sent on 13 April 1961 new to the Central Ordnance Depot, Bicester. On 3 June 1961 it was transferred to the Central Ordnance Depot, Donnington, where it remained until December 1989. Purchased privately, it was moved to Chinnor on 9 October 1991 and was named *Iris*.

Baguley 0–4–0 diesel-mechanical was built in 1952 for Ind Coope Brewery, Burton-on-Trent. It became their No. 1 and worked until the mid-1960s, when it was purchased by Tarmac Roadstone for use at Middle Peak Quarry, Wirksworth, Derbyshire. Purchased privately, it moved to Chinnor on 14 September 1990 and is named *Boris*.

Class 117 DMU No. 117418, comprising driving cars No. 51351 and No. 51397 and intermediate trailer No. 59501, was built by Pressed Steel Ltd, Glasgow, in 1960. It was allocated to the Western Region and was chiefly based at Reading and Old Oak Common. Purchased privately, the set arrived at Chinnor on 2 November 1994.

The association has four ex-BR coaches, one LNWR brake-third, an LMS inspection saloon, two GWR brake vans, a 'Shoc' van, a box van, a flat truck, a low-loading wagon and a BP Petrol tank. Mobile plant includes a 1960 rail-mounted Coles crane and a Wickham petrol trolley.

In 1995 a diesel-hauled service worked every Saturday, Sunday and Bank holiday from Easter until the end of October, and weekends in December for 'Santa and Mince Pie' specials. There was a normal service of six trains on each operating day and seven on days from May till September. In May 1995, 0–4–2T No. 1466 from the Great Western Society at Didcot made a special visit. It was the first steam engine to run on the line for 33 years.

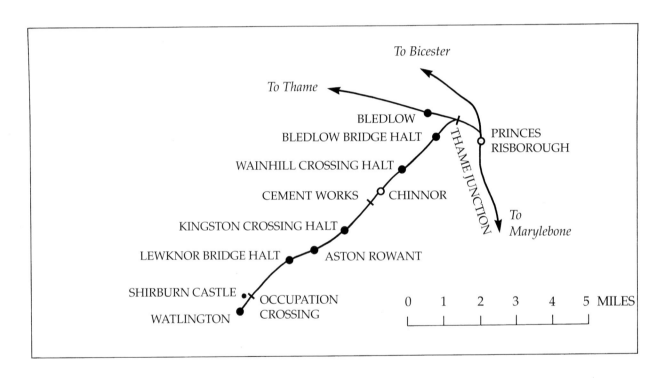

Wainhill Crossing Halt, view Down. Notice the low-level platform, which is hardly any higher than the rails. A notice below the nameboard warns 'Do Not Alight Here'.

6.5.95 Author

A tank engine working bunker-first arrives at Chinnor with an Up passenger train. The ground frame is on the left and beyond the passenger station is the goods shed. The future site of the cement factory is still green fields.

c. 1905 Lens of Sutton

A Down passenger train approaches Chinnor, headed by an 0–6–0ST. The ground frame is on the right. The van in the loading dock is No. 37655.

c. 1905 Author's collection

A 57XX class 0–6–0PT, No. 5755, leaves Chinnor with a Down train and passes the cement works. The Chiltern Hills are in the background.

1957 N.C. Simmons

A 1 ton yard crane at Chinnor. To its right is the weighbridge and weighbridge hut – a feature of many stations. Notice the white-painted bullhead rails, which mark the edge of the weighbridge.

June 1963 D.J. Hyde

An 8750 class 0–6–0PT, No. 4650, leaving Chinnor with a Down train. Its headlamp is carried in an unorthodox position.

29.6.57 E. Wilmshurst

Chinnor, view from station to cement works. A ground frame hut is on the left and a class 08 diesel-electric 0–6–0 *Haversham*.

6.5.95 Author

A 14XX class 0–4–2T, No. 1466, on loan from Didcot Railway Centre, returns to Chinnor with the 11.45.

6.5.95 Author

Grounded Cambrian Railways coach body on the rebuilt Chinnor station platform. Originally No. 247, the coach was carried on six wheels.

6.5.95 Author

Chinnor & Princes Risborough Railway logo carried on a coach.
6.5.95 Author

A 57XX class 0–6–0PT, No. 5755, approaches Kingston Crossing Halt with an Up train. The crossing keeper's lodge is on the right.

1957 N.C. Simmons

A 'Metro' class 2–4–0T at Aston Rowant with a Down train.

c. 1905 Lens of Sutton

Aston Rowant station. This photograph was probably taken after the station was closed to passenger traffic. The building is made of red brick and flint. The timber-built goods shed is beyond.

c. 1957 Lens of Sutton

An 8750 class 0–6–0PT, No. 3697, of 81B (Slough) shed. The engine is hauling autotrailer No. W181W (ex-steam railmotor No. 54) at Aston Rowant, and is working the 2.32 p.m. Princes Risborough to Watlington service. The track has been newly relaid on concrete sleepers, the old timber ones being piled at the end of the platform. Notice the handpump, used to raise water from the station well.

8.9.56 Hugh Ballantyne

Lewknor Bridge Halt, view Down. Concrete fence posts are stacked on either side of the waiting shelter, which needs attention.

12.5.56 E. Wilmshurst

Watlington, view Up. This photograph was taken before the platform in the foreground was extended, and before September 1906, when the engine shed to the right was burned down, never to be replaced. Part of the carriage shed can be seen on the far right. Enamel advertisements fixed to battens on the side of the station building include Crossley's Patent Gas Plants and Sutton's Seeds. Notice the three milk churns and the station garden. Beyond the low signal-box at the platform end a Down train approaches.

c. 1905 Paul Strong collection

A 2021 class 0–6–0PT, No. 2055, and an autotrailer at Watlington. Notice that the locomotive's cab is lower than the coach roof. The tarpaulin on the cab roof could be rolled down in bad weather and when going bunker-first, to give some measure of protection. The platform is in the left foreground.

17.6.39 H.C. Casserley

Watlington, view to buffers. Notice the water tank and goods shed centre, the loading gauge on the right and the brake van, left on the main line.

c. 1951 J.H. Russell

A 57XX class 0–6–0PT, No. 5766 (81B Slough), at Watlington, uncoupling before running round the autotrailer. The carriage is on the right. Notice the steps for carriage cleaning.

July 1957 P.Q. Treloar

No. 5766 has moved forward to clear the points and will reverse along the run-round road.

July 1957 P.Q. Treloar

No. 5766 has its tanks filled with water. Notice the 10 m.p.h. permanent way restriction board, stabilized by two cast-iron chairs.

July 1957 P.Q. Treloar

Pen Farm Siding to Oxford

The broad gauge branch from Princes Risborough to Oxford was authorized by the Wycombe Railway (Extension to Oxford & Aylesbury) Act of 28 June 1861. Built by contractor Thomas Tredwell and leased by the GWR, it opened to Thame on 1 August 1862. The first train, carrying directors and shareholders, arrived at 3.00 p.m. drawn by *Sunbeam*, a 'Sun' class 2–2–2. The line was opened to the public the following day. Work on the remainder of the line to Kennington Junction south of Oxford had begun by December 1862. Once work was completed, it opened on 24 October 1864 and the company amalgamated with the GWR as from 1 February 1867. The line was given over to the engineers on Tuesday 23 August 1870 and reopened for standard gauge passengers on Thursday 1 October 1870. Standard gauge goods trains commenced a few days later.

Following the granting of an Act for constructing a new line from Old Oak Common Junction to High Wycombe in 1897, in 1900 powers were obtained for substantial improvements to the Thame branch. A new line 5½ miles in length was to be built, avoiding Horspath Tunnel. Also, track levels were to be improved and the branch doubled. In the event, these improvements were never carried out as the directors considered a direct line from High Wycombe to Aynho Junction to be a better proposition.

The line closed to passengers from 7 January 1963, remaining open for parcels and goods, but the state of Horspath Tunnel caused the section from Morris Cowley to Thame to be closed as the repair cost of approximately £60,000 was quite uneconomic. Through freight and parcels were intended to cease on 6 February 1967, but due to main line heavy engineering work on Sundays, Paddington to Birkenhead trains were diverted via Thame and Oxford to Banbury. The section was closed completely on 1 May 1967.

Both ends of the line continued to flourish: the western end dealt principally with cars; the eastern end with oil. At peak times Thame received block oil trains from Llandarcy, the Isle of Grain and Ripple Lane, two to three trains running to the terminal daily. Eventually a pipeline was laid to Thame so that oil could be pumped there instead of being taken by rail. On 21 March 1991, Class 37/7 No. 37709 worked the 13.20 Ripple Lane to Thame light engine and returned with eight loaded 100 ton TEA tanks. This 16.50 ex-Thame was the last booked train to use the branch. The tanks were loaded as they were carrying surplus heating oil back to North Thameside. Two more trains visited the line on 10 and 12 April, hauled by No. 47369 and No. 47223, each forming a 16.50 Thame to Ripple Lane returning surplus oil stock. In May 1995 the track was still in place, though many sleepers had been lifted at the Princes Risborough end.

The first feature on the branch in Oxfordshire was Pen Farm Siding facing Down trains. Opened at the commencement of the line, by 1933 the siding was rarely used and it was removed on 18 September 1939. Just under a mile beyond was Towersey Halt, opened on 5 June 1933. The sleeper-built platform was surmounted by a corrugated iron pagoda waiting shelter.

Thame was the principal station on the branch and, befitting its importance, had a timber-built train shed 90 ft by 46 ft, which partly covered the length of two platforms. The station buildings of brick were on the Up side. Also on this side was a goods shed and yard with four sidings, while behind the Down platform was a siding where extensive cattle pens were built in 1931. The station's stables were converted into a lorry garage by replacing one end-wall with doors. One signal at the east end of the station was on a lattice post, which was most unusual for the GWR. West of the station, new sidings were laid for Shell-Mex & BP traffic, commencing on 6 January 1958. Thame was closed to goods on 10 October 1966 and the signal-box was shut on 17 November 1968, from which date the branch from Princes Risborough to Thame was worked as a siding. West of Thame, a large 'Change of Gradient' board, which was illuminated at night, was placed on the Up side.

Tiddington had a single platform on which there was a timber building with a slated roof. The sidings in the yard were worked from a full-sized signal-box, though there were no signals. Milk traffic and agricultural machinery from Messrs Jarmain's works at Haseley were despatched by rail. The station closed to goods on 30 December 1963.

Over the weekend of 21–2 October 1961 a single-span pre-assembled bridge weighing 90 tons was placed in position at Wheatley, crossing what was to be the dual carriageway of the A40. Designed to match the existing span, the bridge was the first of its kind to be erected in the country. It was manufactured at the Chepstow works of Messrs Fairfield Ltd. An existing abutment was reconstructed to form a central pier between the two carriageways. Buses replaced trains for two days until the work was complete. When the Morris Cowley to Thame section of the line closed, this bridge was recycled to Cwmbach near Aberdare, where it spans a river.

Wheatley Viaduct, 44 yd in length and consisting of a steel girder bridge with an intermediate pier, crossed the River Thame. The line then rose at 1 in 84 to the passing loop at Wheatley station a mile beyond. The buildings were of brick and the small goods shed was sited on the passenger platform. It became a coal depot only, until its complete closure on 1 May 1967.

The line passed through Horspath Tunnel, which was 524 yd in length, and beyond was Horspath Halt. The halt, 150 ft long, first opened on 1 February 1908 with the introduction of the railmotor service. It closed on 23 March 1915 as a wartime economy measure. At a cost of about £200 a new halt, 44 yd to the west, was opened on 5 June 1933, with the platform of old sleepers perched high on an embankment. The line descended on a gradient of 1 in 87 towards Garsington Bridge Halt, which was opened on 1 February 1908 on the west side of Garsington Road. It closed on 22 March 1915. East of the halt a mine factory opened during the First World War. This was served by a siding. In 1926, as the Morris and the associated Pressed Steel works expanded, a siding was laid. This was joined by six others two years later. Morris Cowley station, a single platform with a timber office building, opened on 24 September 1928 on the same site as Garsington Bridge Halt. Because there was only one platform, the loop could only cross one passenger and one goods train, or two goods trains. When the station closed to passengers on 7 January 1963, it was said to be taking more in car parking fees than train fares.

Today things are very much alive at Railfreight's Morris Cowley International Terminal. The 20,000 sq. ft warehouse was opened on 9 May 1984 by David Mitchell MP,

Parliamentary Secretary for Transport, as part of a joint project between BR and F.C. Bennett. (Bennett's later became United Transport Logistics Ltd.) Some years ago, locomotive No. 47218 was named *United Transport Europe* in this warehouse. A Connectrail service brings chipboard by rail from Austria and Perrier water from France, which is unloaded in the warehouse where it is stored before being distributed by road.

Principal traffic at the eleven-road yard is Rover cars, the transport of which is organized by MAT Transauto Ltd (Machinery & Technical Transport), which has a fenced compound capable of storing 1,100 cars adjacent to the depot. Cars are lined up in the compound for despatch on trains to Southampton, Purfleet and Italy, cars for the latter two destinations travelling via Washwood Heath. The terminal handled some 70,000 cars by rail in 1994.

The train service varies to suit the traffic. As an illustration, the service from 20 March 1995 was as follows:

Depart		Arrive
02.55	SO Washwood Heath – Morris Cowley	05.30
02.05	MSX Longbridge East – Morris Cowley	05.35
07.30	MSX Morris Cowley – Southampton West Docks	11.03
06.20	MWFO Washwood Heath – Morris Cowley	09.10
10.15	MWFO Morris Cowley – Washwood Heath	12.33
13.31	FSX Longbridge East – Morris Cowley	17.23
20.15	FSX Morris Cowley – Washwood Heath	22.33

The trains of car wagons that go to Washwood Heath are combined with others from Longbridge, from where they travel direct through the Channel Tunnel to Milan. Similarly, other trains from Longbridge are combined at Morris Cowley with wagons loaded with cars at Morris Cowley before the combined train is despatched to Southampton West Docks for shipment. Some cars arriving at Morris Cowley are for MAT delivery by road to Milton Trading Estate near Didcot.

MAT has its own carriage and wagon maintenance staff at Morris Cowley, and Mainline Freight Operating staff check that any required work has been carried out satisfactorily.

Two class 08 shunters from Saltley depot are outstationed at Morris Cowley for shunting. In March 1995 these were No. 08751 and No. 08946. Maintenance staff are sent by road from Saltley. The engines are filled from a road tanker, which arrives every three to four months, and as the same fuel is used for office heating, this is brought in the same load. The driver for class 08 comes from the Mainline Freight Operating Company at Didcot, and on arrival at Oxford station is collected by Railfreight Distribution (RfD) van, which takes him to Morris Cowley and returns him to the station afterwards. The same van is also used for conveying a shunter to Hinksey when a locomotive needs to run round there, the other shunter travelling down on the engine. After the locomotive has proceeded to the other end of the train, both shunters return in the van.

At Morris Cowley each of the class 08s is used on alternate days to keep the fuel level of each approximately the same. Owing to the curves and resulting poor vision, three radios are used when shunting: one for each of the two shunters and one for the driver. A shunter says to a driver approaching a raft of wagons: '30 ft to go; 25 ft . . . 6 ft; 4 ft; 3 ft; 2 ft; 1 ft; 6 inches. Stop.'

Morris Cowley Works had rail sidings and used a John Fowler & Co diesel-mechanical

Sleeper-built Towersey Halt, view Down, which is lit by two oil lamps.

c. 1960 Lens of Sutton

0–4–0 built in 1955. It was sent to Longbridge in 1971. In 1965 the British Motor Corporation (BMC) opened a warehouse complex distributing spares. It used a John Fowler diesel-hydraulic 0–4–0 named *BMC Services Ltd No. 1*, and when rail traffic ceased in 1971 it was transferred to Cowley Works prior to being sent to Longbridge. In 1960, when a diesel locomotive was being repaired, the BMC hired Western Region 0–4–2T No. 1444. The Pressed Steel Co. Ltd had a new Fowler diesel-mechanical 0–4–0 in 1935, which was subsequently joined by five more from the same builder and also one diesel-hydraulic. During the Second World War the diesels were augmented by an 0–4–0ST, which was built by Andrew Barclay. Rail traffic within the works ceased in July 1975, when the newest engine was transferred to the company's plant at Swindon.

Littlemore had a single platform and two sidings. The County Lunatic Asylum had its own private siding for coal, which was reached via a turntable in the yard. The siding agreement terminated on 1 July 1968 and the station closed to goods on 21 June 1971. To the west, a long siding ran parallel for about 500 yd to serve two petrol depots and sandpits. The BP oil depot had accommodation for a maximum of twelve 32 ton wagons, and between one and four deliveries were made each week. The last oil train ran on 23 February 1993.

The branch line descends at 1 in 93 and crosses the Thames by the 81 yd long Kennington Viaduct, a bow-string girder bridge supported on two intermediate piers. Owing to subsidence the bridge was replaced by another, slightly downstream, on 29 July 1923. Immediately beyond was the 150 ft long halt, which was opened on 1 February 1908 and closed on 22 March 1915. Its original name was to have been Oxford Sewage Bridge Halt, but this was changed to the sweeter-sounding Iffley Halt. The branch joins the Didcot to Oxford main line at Kennington Junction. In conjunction with the Oxford Panel Box the single line token is picked up from a lineside box here.

The branch was used as an alternative route to Oxford and Birmingham, and was capable of taking all engines except 'Kings'. It was regularly used when engineering works were carried out on the Paddington–Bicester–Birmingham main line.

In the nineteenth century the line was worked by 0–4–2Ts and 2–4–0Ts on passenger trains with Armstrong Standard and Dean Goods 0–6–0s on freight. In the 1920s, 'Bulldog' and 'County' 4–4–0s appeared on passenger trains and 61XX class 2–6–2Ts. GWR diesel railcars worked from 1935 until 1957. During the Second World War, USA 2–8–0s worked oil trains to Thame, initially piloted from Kennington Junction by an 0–6–0PT. However, when it was realized the seriousness of a breakaway on the rising gradient of 1 in 80, assistance was given at the rear. Following D-Day, LNER B12 class 4–6–0s hauled ambulance trains to Wheatley, patients being conveyed by road to the military hospital at Holton Park. In BR times 'Britannia' Pacifics, Standard Class 9F 2–10–0s and 75000 class 4MT 4–6–0s, 'Patriots', 'Jubilees' and 'Royal Scots' appeared on Washwood Heath car trains. Steam finished when Oxford shed closed on 3 January 1966.

Latterly, oil trains to Thame were worked by Class 37/7 of the North Thameside petroleum fleet and occasionally a Class 47. In 1986 a variety of locomotives worked to Morris Cowley: Classes 20, 25, 31, 45, 47, 50, 56 and 58. Today trains are worked by Class 47s.

In 1887, between Princes Risborough and Oxford, six Down and four Up trains were run on weekdays and two each way on Sundays, taking 55 minutes for the distance of 21 miles. By 1910 the service offered seven each way plus a railmotor from Oxford to Wheatley and back, another motor running from Oxford to Thame. Two trains still ran on Sundays. By 1922 the extra services were centred on Princes Risborough rather than Oxford. Five passenger trains ran each way, plus three railmotors worked from Princes Risborough to Thame and back. This frequency varied little until passenger traffic was withdrawn.

Some trains ran through from Oxford to Paddington via Thame and Bourne End, and it was not unknown for passengers at Oxford who were intending to catch an express via Reading to enter a train labelled 'Paddington' and unwittingly suffer a protracted journey.

In 1933 a workmen's through train ran from Banbury, departing at 6.00 a.m., to Morris Cowley, arriving at 7.08 a.m., with a return working departing from Morris Cowley at 5.08 p.m. and arriving at Banbury at 6.06 p.m. On Saturdays the departure was at 12.10 p.m. and the train ran to Kingham with a connection to Banbury.

The 1933 timetable showed two goods trains each way, plus one Oxford to Thame and back and two Oxford to Morris Cowley and back. In 1959, five through goods trains ran over the branch, including some to Worcester.

The branch featured in *Memoirs of a Stationmaster* by Ernest J. Simmons. Published in 1879, this book gives a remarkably vivid picture of life at Thame more than 130 years ago, before the extension was opened to Oxford.

Referring to his temporary superintendent, Mr Besant, Simmons wrote:

Mine being a terminus, from which there was no chance of his returning for at least three hours, he very rarely paid me a visit, and I reigned almost supreme at Thame station. As I went to and from my house to the station the little boys in the street used to say, 'That's the stationmaster,' and on Sunday quite a tribe of country people walked in to see the trains start, for the railway was only just opened, and very few country people had travelled by a train. Our engine driver, for we only had one, had quite extinguished their admiration of 'the Village Blacksmiths', and, as our station was worked as a branch line from Princes Risborough to Thame, the plough boys saved up

WYCOMBE, AYLESBURY, THAME AND OXFORD BRANCH.

Passengers may have to change Carriages at Taplow. For Intermediate Stations on Main Line, see Pages 16, 17, 18, 19.

Distance	DOWN.	Week Days.											Sundays.				
				U ‡ G					E		A	B		G		A	B
		1, 2, 3 class.	1 & 2 class.	1, 2, 3 class.	1 & 2 class.	1 & 2 class.	1 & 2 class.	1 & 2 class	1 & 2 class.	1, 2, 3 class.	1 & 2 class.	1, 2, 3 class.	1, 2, 3 class.	1, 2, 3 class.	1, 2, 3 class.	1 & 2 class.	1, 2, 3 class
		a.m.	a.m.	a.m.	a.m.	p.m.	p.m.	p.m.	p.m.	p.m.	p.m.	p.m.	a.m.	a.m.	p.m.	p.m.	p.m.
—	**London** Pad. Stat.	.	.	8 0	10 25	12 20	.	.	5 0	.	7 0	8 10	.	8 40	.	7 0	8 10
	London Victoria	..	..	7 33	9 55	11 47	..	..	..	..	6 32	..	..	..	..	6 10	..
	London Kensington	...	...	7 55	10 18	12 10	...	...	...	...	6 52	...	...	...	...	6 30	...
22¾	Taplow Arr.	.	.	9 0	11 27	1 32	.	.	5 39	.	8 6	8 50	.	9 43	.	8 6	8 50
	Taplow Dep.	..	..	9 5	11 32	1 35	..	...	5 41	..	8 55	8 55	..	9 45	..	8 55	8 55
24¾	Maidenhead (BoyneH.)	...	...	9 12	11 39	1 42	...	...	5 49	...	9 3	9 3	...	9 52	...	9 3	9 3
27¼	Cookham	.	.	9 19	11 45	1 47	.	.	5 55	.	9 10	9 10	.	9 59	.	9 10	9 10
28¾	Marlow Road	..	..	9 25	11 51	1 52	..	..	6 1	..	9 17	9 17	..	10 5	..	9 17	9 17
30	Woburn Green	...	...	9 31	11 56	1 57	...	...	6 6	...	9 22	9 22	...	10 10	...	9 22	9 22
31½	Loudwater	.	.	9 36	12 1	2 2	.	.	6 11	.	9 27	9 27	.	10 15	.	9 27	9 27
34¼	**High Wycombe** Arr.	..	..	9 44	12 8	2 8	..	..	6 17	..	9 33	9 33	..	10 22	..	9 33	9 33
	High Wycombe Dep.	7 5	...	9 50	12 10	2 10	...	...	6 20	...	9 35	9 35	...	10 25	...	9 35	9 35
36¾	West Wycombe	7 11	.	9 56	—	2 16	.	.	6 26	.	9 41	9 41	.	10 31	.	9 41	9 41
42¾	Princes Risboro' Arr.	7 23	..	10 7	12 25	2 27	..	.	6 36	..	9 52	9 52	..	10 42	..	9 52	9 52
—	R'bro' (Dep. for Aylesb.)	7 45	9 30	10 11	12 32	2 31	3 15	5 16	6 40	7 30	9 55	9 55	7 15	10 47	6 45	9 56	9 56
49¾	Aylesbury Arrive	8 0	9 45	10 25	12 47	2 45	3 30	5 30	6 55	7 45	10 10	10 10	7 30	11 0	7 0	10 10	10 10
—	R'bro. (Dp. for Thame and Oxford.)	7 25	.	10 9	12 30	2 29	.	.	6 38	.	.	.	.	10 45	.	9 54	9 54
44¾	Bledlow	7 30	..	10 14	12 35	2 34	..	..	6 43	..	..	..	..	10 50	..	9 59	9 59
48¼	Thame Arr.	7 38	...	10 22	12 42	2 45	...	...	6 50	...	...	...	...	10 58	...	10 5	10 5
	Thame Dep.	7 40	.	10 24	12 45	2 57	.	.	6 51	.	.	.	.	11 0	.	10 7	10 7
55¾	Wheatley	7 55	..	10 38	1 2	3 12	..	..	7 9	..	..	..	..	11 15	.	10 24	10 24
60	Littlemore	8 5	...	10 48	1 12	3 22	...	...	7 19	...	...	...	...	11 25	..	10 34	10 34
63¼	**Oxford** Arrive	8 15	.	10 55	1 20	3 30	.	.	7 28		.	.	.	11 35	...	10 45	10 45

Distance	UP. Starting from	Week Days,											Sundays				
			E	‡ E	F				E			‡ G	G		‡ G		
		1, 2, 3 class.	1 & 2 class.	1, 2, 3 class.	1 & 2 class.	1, 2, 3 class.	1 & 2 class	1 & 2 class.	1, & 2 class.	1 & 2 class.	1 & 2 class.	1, 2, 3 class.	1, 2, 3 class.	1, 2, 3 class.	1, 2, 3 class.	1, 2, 3 class.	
		a.m.	a.m.	a.m.	a.m.	a.m.	p.m.	p.m.	p.m.	p.m.	p.m.	p.m.	a.m.	a.m.	p.m.	p.m.	
—	**Oxford** Depart.	.	.	.	8 35	.	11 30	.	2 15	4 20	.	6 15	6 20	.	5 40	.	.
3¼	Littlemore	..	..	..	8 44	..	11 40	..	2 25	4 30	..	6 24	6 30	..	5 50	..	..
7½	Wheatley	...	...	...	8 54	...	11 53	...	2 35	4 40	...	6 34	6 40	...	6 0	...	...
15	Thame Arr.	.	.	.	9 8	.	12 9	.	2 50	4 55	.	6 49	6 53	.	6 15	.	.
	Thame Dep.	.	.	.	9 10	.	12 12	.	2 55	4 57	.	7 5	6 55	.	6 20	.	.
19	Bledlow	..	..	..	9 18	..	12 23	..	3 5	5 7	..	7 15	7 4	..	6 30	..	..
24¼	R'bro' (Ar. from Thame)	...	...	...	9 23	...	12 27	...	3 10	5 12	...	7 20	7 9	...	6 38	...	...
28	Aylesbury Dep.	7 10	7 30	7 30	9 5	9 50	12 10	2 10	2 50	4 55	6 20	7 5	6 50	10 15	6 20	9 35	.
—	R'bro' (Ar. from Aylesb.)	7 23	7 43	7 43	9 20	10 5	12 25	2 24	3 5	5 9	6 34	7 20	7 5	10 30	6 33	9 50	..
—	Princes Risboro' Dep.	.	7 45	7 45	9 20	.	12 29	.	3 13	5 15	.	7 25	7 12	.	6 43	.	.
26¼	West Wycombe	..	7 57	7 57	9 38	..	12 42	..	3 28	5 28	..	7 38	7 24	..	6 55	..	..
29	**High Wycombe** Arr.	...	8 4	8 4	9 44	...	12 48	...	3 35	5 35	...	7 45	7 30	...	7 8	...	...
	High Wycombe Dep.	.	8 7	8 7	9 47	.	12 50	.	3 38	—	.	7 48	7 34	.	7 13	.	.
31¾	Loudwater	..	8 15	8 15	..	..	12 57	..	3 45	..	..	7 55	7 42	..	7 21	..	..
33	Woburn Green	...	8 20	8 20	...	...	1 2	...	3 52	...	...	8 2	7 47	...	7 28	...	...
34¾	Marlow Road	.	8 25	8 25	9 58	.	1 7	.	3 57	.	.	8 10	7 52	.	7 34	.	.
36	Cookham	..	8 32	8 32	..	..	1 12	..	4 2	..	..	8 16	7 58	..	7 42	..	..
38½	Maidenhead (Boyne H.)	...	8 39	8 39	...	...	1 17	...	4 7	...	...	8 22	8 4	...	7 52	...	...
40	Taplow Arr.	.	8 48	8 48	10 10	.	1 25	.	4 15	.	.	8 30	8 12	.	8 0	.	.
	Taplow Dep.	..	9 0	9 0	10 13	..	1 30	..	4 18	..	..	8 42	8 15	..	8 5	..	..
68¼	**London** Kensington	.	.	10 16	.	.	2 30	.	5 45	.	.	.	10 2	.	.	.	.
	London Victoria	..	..	10 35	...	..	2 50	..	6 2	..	..	..	10 23	..	..	..	..
	London Pad. Stat.	...	9 40	10 15	11 0	...	2 20	...	5 25	...	...	9 55	9 30	...	9 15	...	...

A 3rd Class from all Stations except Paddington to the Wycombe and Aylesbury Branch.
B 3rd Class from London only to the Wycombe and Aylesbury Branch.
D Third Class from Stations between Littlemore and Bledlow inclusive to London and intermediate Stations; also, 3rd Class from Oxford to Stations up to Marlow Road inclusive.
E Horses and Carriages are not conveyed between London and Taplow by these Trains.
F Third Class from Stations between Littlemore and Bledlow inclusive to London and intermediate Stations, also Third Class from Oxford to Stations up to Marlow Road inclusive.
G 1st and 2nd Class only between London and Oxford.
U Horses and Carriages not conveyed to or from the Wycombe and Thame Branches by this Train, but must be sent from London and other Stations by the 7.5 a.m. Train if intended to go by the 9.10 a.m. from Taplow.
‡ First and Second Class only between London and Taplow.

The timetable for June 1865.

their money and had a ride from Thame to Princes Risborough on a Sunday, for the novelty of the thing. I have booked as many as fifty of these youngsters on one Sunday, who had no other object in travelling.

My first pantomime did not delight me more than this ride delighted them, and they walked back eight and nine miles to whistle and plough, and talk about 'how the trees and hedges rund along when 'us' was in that thaire train', and how 'it frit I, when she went under the arch.

One Sunday morning a countrywoman of about fifty years in age knocked on Ernest Simmons' office door:

'Good marning, sir; bin you the stationmaster?' said my visitor. I assured her that I was, when she continued – 'Please, sir, I be going by train, and do you know, sir, I've never bin. I *do hope* I shall go safe! I be going to Aylesbury to see my darter Betty, and she's a comin down by the London & North Western Railway, and we be going to spend the day there at a sister's as I've got, and then she's a going back to sarvice, and I be a coming home; and I do hope, sir, as you'll see me safe, for I be most afraid on't.'

Poor old soul, she trembled all over, so I took her into the waiting room and bade her sit down; but she reminded me of my own sittings in a dentist's room, when waiting to have a tooth out, for she was evidently ill at ease.

She asked to wait in his office and inquired: '"Please, sir, do you tickut me here, or when I gets there?" I took her back to the office, gave her a ticket and instructions as to changing trains at Princes Risborough for Aylesbury.' In due course the train started. Stationmaster Simmons continued working in his office. Then, seeing a Down train signalled, he went to meet it. Who should get out but the old woman, who exclaimed:

'Lor' me, I be at Thame again, and my darter Betty's at Aylesbury.' You may be sure that I blamed the Guard, but he said that to begin with, she rushed out at the first station, and that he had to stop the train to get her in again; that when he got to Princes Risborough he took her and told her where to wait; that he had his parcels and milk cans to see to, and that it was not his fault if she rushed about like a maniac at the sound of every whistle, and made a fool of herself. He did not see her in his train or he should have been only too glad to get rid of her.

Poor old thing, she cried bitterly; waited all day at the station and went again by the four o'clock train, on which occasion I booked her as a parcel, putting a label on her umbrella, and handing the guard a way bill of 'One woman for Aylesbury.'

She found her daughter, spent two hours with her, and returned by the last train, but vehemently declared as she went home, 'Never no more trains for me, if I can't go in a waggin I'll stay at home till I be berrid, that I will.'

On one occasion Simmons forwarded the single line staff as usual by a certain train, quite forgetting that an extra was running that month and that he should have kept the staff and despatched the first with a ticket. It was a serious mistake for which he was liable to be called before the Board of Directors, so he went to a friend's stables to borrow a horse. The only mount available was an unbroken colt. Deciding that riding the youngster was the lesser of the two evils, he galloped quite out of control off to Princes Risborough, 8 miles away. At the station yard he got a lad to hold the colt while he went to the unattended booking office and took the staff off its hook. He trotted and cantered back to Thame, and

. . . four minutes to the appointed time, I walked leisurely into the booking office at Thame station as if nothing had happened. The people were a little uneasy about their tickets it is true, but there were not more than twelve of them. They were soon booked and I was about to start the train when Tom Burley came rushing into the office like a wild man.

'Mr Simmons', said he, 'I've bin to your house and all over the town for you. Do you know, sir, you sent the staff away by that last train, and that this un can't start? I see you give it to the guard.' 'Nonsense', I replied, at the same time producing it from my pocket. Tom Burley stared like one in a trance.

Only one person at the station did I let into the secret of my being scarcely able to walk for some days, and that person was Tom Burley, whose admiration for my exploit was constantly showing itself in some small, but kindly manner. He would not let me move from the office stool if he could help it.

James Sandy, the branch engine driver, was fond of beer and fond of showing off when driving. As long as 'Mad' Sandy was the only driver on the line he did little harm, but when the extension to Oxford was being built, a ballast train also used the line.

One evening Simmons was waiting for the Down ballast train to come before despatching the Up passenger train when he heard Sandy's engine whistle. At first he thought that Sandy was just running the engine up and down to pump water into the boiler, but Simmons was horrified to see that he had started off with about 45 passengers aboard.

Tom Burley was sent to summon both of the Thame doctors to the station to treat the expected casualties and all waited. Breaking the silence was the two brake whistles of the engines. No crash was heard and then the sound of an ordinary whistle told them that one train was about to start.

Although the passengers were safe, one life was lost. A crossing keeper saw Sandy's unauthorized train approaching and closed a crossing gate in the hope that it would warn him. The ballast engine blew its brake whistle and 'Mad' Sandy blew his, but to no purpose as he had left the guard, who would have applied the coach brakes, behind at Thame. The gate was shattered, a piece piercing the wall of the crossing keeper's cottage and killing him. The trains stopped 10 yd apart.

The extension was not an unmitigated blessing:

The Thame people clamoured loudly for the new line to be opened to Oxford, which expected event was to be an immense boon, but which has, in reality, worked against them by bringing the trade of the town into competition with that of a much larger one, and by affording means of escape for commercial travellers and others who were obliged in the old days to stay the night. Railways drain small towns and feed large ones.

In those early days, the risk of accident was always present:

I had no proper signalman, and the duty of shifting the signals devolved on a porter, named 'Brook', a young man, who had several other duties, whose negligence was often the subject of remonstrance from me.

The new line was already used as a short cut for an express goods train, which ran through our station 'full steam'.

The passenger train from Princes Risborough to Oxford stood on a side line whilst the express goods ran through, and after it had passed, the points communicating with the main line were opened and the passenger train proceeded.

Thus it depended on the closing or opening of these points as to the line on which the approaching express goods train ran.

My readers will thus be enabled to see that had these points been left open the approaching train would run into the passenger train standing on that side line, instead of running safely through the station.

These points were a matter of great anxiety to me, for they were always being opened and shut for the ballast train, and I knew that 'Porter Broom', who had the care of them, was not to be depended upon.

That day I was booking the train and brooding over my troubles at home, when

'Broom' came in with his goods consignment notes. I never saw 'Broom' without refreshing his memory, and, from habit I suppose, I said to him, 'Have you put that signal right (for there was only one signal instead of two) for the express goods?'

'Yes sir', replied Broom.

'And did you put the points right and lock them?' I further enquired.

'They were right this morning', replied Broom.

Not a moment's hesitation, not a second thought or enquiry, I did not even stop to close my cash drawer, but I knocked a passenger over who stood in the way of my shoulder, and I was running, not for my life, but for the lives of others, to the points, for I knew that if Broom had not put them right *since* the morning they must be wrong. The signal was indeed 'all right', but the points were 'all wrong', and the safety of the unconscious load of passengers depended on my turning them before the express train got there. She was coming 'full steam' and I was going 'full steam', Broom, too, was coming behind me, but I had distanced him, for I could run.

If you had been an observer of the race I think you would have decided against my chance of success, but the excitement of the moment lent me the wings of lightning, as it were.

The train was coming like a charge of cavalry, the points were between us. I had to stand on the line where the train would pass if I missed the handle. It was death or victory.

Another moment and I should have been a mangled corpse or the train would have passed the station in safety.

I need not tell you it was the latter, I had turned the points and had staggered backwards into a muddy ditch from which Broom extricated me, for my strength had gone.

It was three days before I fairly shook off the reaction of that run for life.

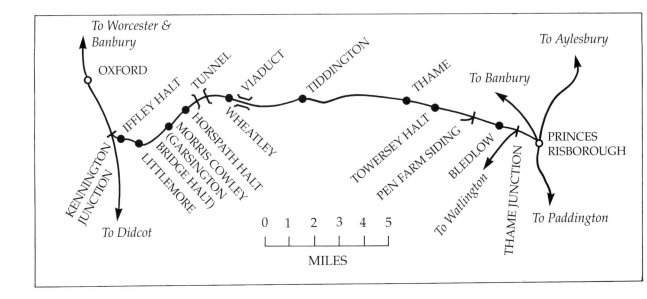

40

View of Thame looking in the Down direction. On the right are the busy goods yard and the goods shed, which is constructed of timber. Beyond is the train shed with the yard crane outside. The signal post in front of the signal-box is of the lattice variety, which is quite rare on the GWR.

c. 1910 Paul Strong collection

Thame, view Up, with both passenger trains headed by 61XX class 2–6–2Ts crossing. On the far right is the cattle pen, the nearby track being set in concrete to allow the water to run into drains. The signal-box is set into the embankment. The lamps are gas-lit and are controlled by pull-wires.

July 1959 Author's collection

An 8750 class 0–6–0PT, No. 9789, and a brake van on the Down line, Thame. Notice that the smoke-box door hinges have been whitened and the cabside number-plate removed prior to withdrawal.

11.8.65 Author

No. 9789 sets off towards Oxford with the 20 ton Eastern Region brake van E235525.

11.8.65 Author

Tiddington station and baulk road, which was originally set to the broad gauge. Wagon No. 44585 is on the left.

c. 1900 D.J. Hyde collection

A Down freight headed by a 61XX class 2–6–2T passes the timber-built station at Tiddington. The signal-box was built in the set-back position to allow for doubling, should this have proved necessary. To the right of the concrete sleepers awaiting laying is the station garden.

14.4.62 E. Wilmshurst

Horspath Halt, perched on an embankment. The station nameboard has lettering on both sides.

c. 1960 Lens of Sutton

A 61XX class 2–6–2T, No. 6124, enters Wheatley with an Up stopping train. The far building on the opposite platform is the goods shed.

6.7.62 Author's collection

'Castle' class 4–6–0 *Westminster Abbey* passes through Wheatley with the 2.10 p.m. Paddington to Birkenhead service. This was a Sunday diversion owing to permanent way work on the direct route through Bicester. This locomotive was rebuilt from the 'Star' class.

11.9.60 Michael Mensing

The timber platform at Morris Cowley, view Down. The wall supporting the platform and the platform edges is made from old sleepers. The passing loop could only be used for crossing two goods trains, or one passenger and one goods train.

c. 1960 Lens of Sutton

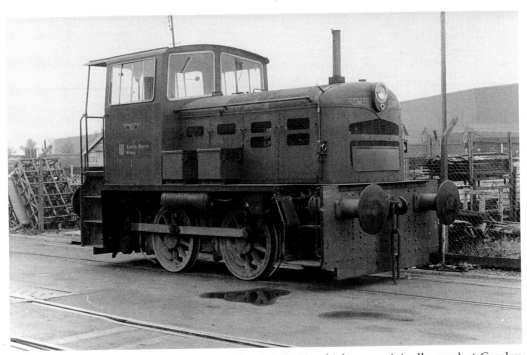

The Austin-Morris Group No. 1 John Fowler 0–4–0DH, which was originally used at Cowley Works, seen here at Pressed Steel Fisher Works, Swindon.

4.8.82 Author

Cars on MAT Cartic wagons. On the far road the wagon roofs have been raised, ready for loading.

21.4.95 Author

Morris Cowley yard shunters No. 08751 (right) and No. 08946.

21.4.95 Author

View from the cab of No. 08946 as it draws out a train of loaded Cartics.

21.4.95 Author

'Hall' class 4–6–0 No. 6934 *Beachamwell Hall* with the 4.10 p.m. Paddington to Birkenhead service, west of Morris Cowley. The train had been diverted because of permanent way works on the Bicester route.

11.9.60 Michael Mensing

Littlemore station and the County Lunatic Asylum, which had its own siding.

c. 1910 Lens of Sutton

Littlemore station, view Down. The siding on the left has chairs laid on Second World War concrete 'pots' to ease the shortage of timber.

c. 1960 Lens of Sutton

Kennington Viaduct across the River Thames, view upstream.

21.4.95 Author

'Bulldog' class 4–4–0 No. 3454 *Skylark* taking the Thame branch at Kennington Junction. Built in January 1910, this engine ceased working in November 1951. Its sister loco, *Seagull*, was withdrawn simultaneously. They were the last remnants of this class. Judging from *Skylark's* condition, this photograph was taken shortly before its retirement.

c. 1951 P.Q. Treloar collection

Blackthorn to Bicester to Souldern Viaducts

This branch, once part of one of the last main lines to be opened, was built to shorten the route from Paddington to Birmingham, which at the turn of the century was via Reading, Didcot and Oxford. Apart from the need for a shorter route to rival the LNWR competition to and from Birmingham, American passenger traffic using Birkenhead had developed and a more direct route was essential. The route planned was a decided improvement. It was 19 miles shorter than via Oxford and 2 miles less than the LNWR's route into Euston.

The first section from Old Oak Common Junction to High Wycombe received parliamentary powers in 1897. Then a joint committee was formed with the Great Central Railway to double and improve the GWR's existing single line from High Wycombe to Princes Risborough and extend it to Ashendon Junction. The Aynho & Ashendon Railway was authorized under the GWR (New Railways) Act of 11 July 1905 to link with the original GWR route at Aynho. It was laid out by W. Armstrong, the GWR's new works engineer. Designed for fast running, it had easy gradients (a ruling gradient of 1 in 193) and gentle curves of not less than 2 miles radius, except at junctions where the minimum curve was a ½ mile radius. Flying junctions were provided at Aynho and Ashendon to avoid conflicting movements.

The contractors, Messrs Scott and Middleton, did not start work until the joint line was fully opened on 2 April 1906. Nearly 3 million cubic yards of clay and rock had to be excavated and deposited to form embankments, and fifty bridges were required. Stations were built in brick to the GWR standard pattern. The line opened to goods on 4 April 1910 and to passengers on 1 July of the same year. It really ceased to be a main line when expresses were withdrawn from the route in 1968, Princes Risborough to Aynho Junction being singled on 4 November 1968.

Entering Oxfordshire the line is on a 7 mile long embankment, which included Blackthorn station, a typical two-road affair, with two goods sidings and a cattle dock in the bay at the north end of the Up platform. No goods shed was provided. An early casualty, the station closed to passengers on 8 June 1953 and to goods on 3 January 1955.

Just ½ mile south-east of Bicester the line crossed the LNWR's Oxford to Cambridge line via a steel bridge. The GWR station was about 1 mile by road from that of the LNWR. Bicester was, and is, a principal station on the line. At one time it had a refreshment room and, most unusually, a changing room for passengers going to or from hunting. 'North' was added to the station name on 26 September 1949. It originally had two platforms and two central roads, but the latter were lifted in May 1968. Both platforms are now signalled for two-way working, the Down platform being the main and the Up platform the loop. Bicester had a sizeable goods yard together with the usual accommodation. There were passing facilities for goods trains of eighty wagons plus an engine and a brake van. To enable the points at each end of the loops to be controlled

Blackthorn, view Up. Notice that about half the width of the platform in the foreground consists of timber decking. The only signal visible is the Down Home, the arm of which is concealed by the footbridge.

c. 1910 Author's collection

from a single signal-box, a siding was provided at the end of each loop. A long train would run through the platform loop into the facing siding to clear the brake van from the main line. It would then set back into the trailing siding until the engine was clear of the main line points. The goods yard became a coal depot only on 19 May 1964. The passenger station was refurbished in July 1991.

Beyond Bicester is a 3½ mile long cutting with a maximum depth of 50 ft, much of it through rock, which required blasting before a steam navvy could lift it into wagons. To blast, holes were drilled 9 ft apart to a depth of 14 in, charged with ammonal and fired by electricity or fuse. Midway along the cutting was Ardley station, which had a four-road layout similar to that of Bicester station. There were two goods sidings and a cattle loading dock. An additional siding was laid in 1928. Ardley, like Bicester, had facilities for handling an eighty-wagon train. The station closed to passengers on 7 January 1963 and to goods on 7 September 1964.

At the far end of the cutting is Ardley Tunnel, which is 1,147 yd in length. When it was bored, in addition to working from each end, four shafts 100 ft deep were sunk, opening eight additional faces. Even so, completion of the brick-lined tunnel took 1½ years. Beyond the tunnel are the two brick-built Souldern Viaducts. No. 1 is 330 yd in length and No. 2 is 400 yd, with eighteen and twenty-four arches respectively, each arch with a span of 40 ft. No. 2 Viaduct carried the line out of Oxfordshire into Northamptonshire.

In its days as a main line, all GWR Standard locomotive classes could be seen here. Today passenger traffic is worked by Class 165/0 Network Turbos. For much of its life as a main line, four Down and five Up stopping trains were run on weekdays only. Today, marketed as the Chiltern Line, twenty trains run each way on weekdays from Marylebone to Banbury, most continuing on to Birmingham, Snow Hill.

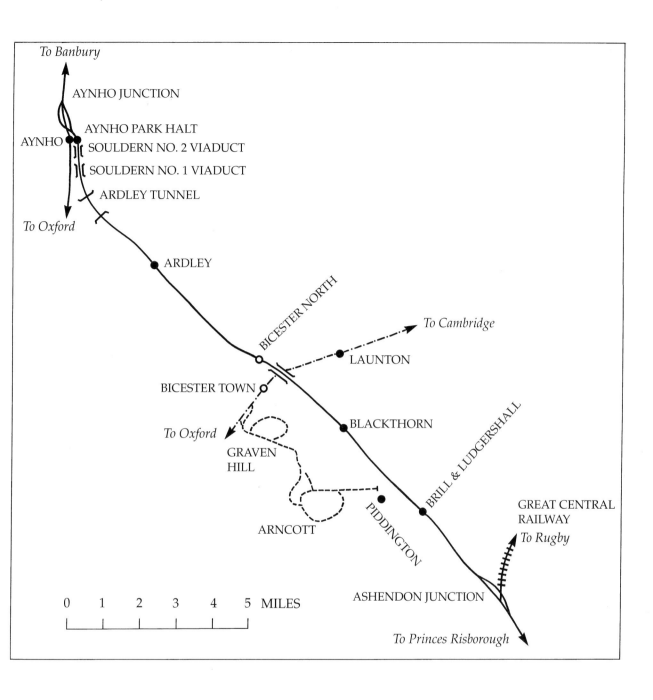

Putting the finishing touches to Bicester station, view Up. The ladder is unusually tall and has about forty rungs.

1910 Author's collection

Bicester station, probably immediately prior to opening as wagons would not normally have been left on the platform road. Notice the goods shed beyond the Down passenger platform and the mass of point rodding on the left.

1910 Lens of Sutton

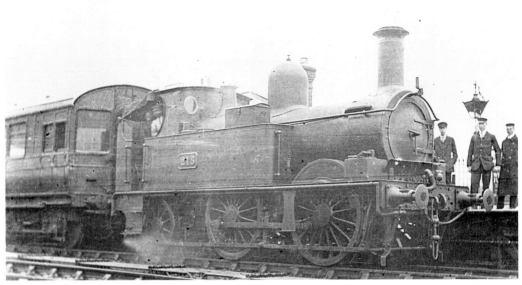

A 517 class 0–4–2T, No. 218, and an autocar at Bicester station. Notice the tarpaulin, which gives minimal shelter for the cab. This engine, which was built in 1876, was withdrawn in 1930.

1918 P.Q. Treloar collection

A 14XX class 0–4–2T, No. 1473, leaving Bicester North station with the 5.00 p.m. Banbury General to Princes Risborough service. The engine had just used the water crane. Autotrailer W236W was built in 1953.

25.8.60 Michael Mensing

A 64XX class 0–6–0PT, No. 6429, taking water at Bicester North station while working the 5.00 p.m. Banbury General service to Princes Risborough. The Down through road has been relaid with flat-bottom rail. The autotrailer is W236W.

31.5.60 Michael Mensing

The slip-coach, detached from the 5.10 p.m. Paddington to Wolverhampton Low Level, entering Bicester North station. On the left is the 4.34 p.m. Paddington to Wolverhampton train, whose engine, No. 5994 *Roydon Hall*, will collect the slip-coach from the centre road and attach it to its own train. The slip-coach is probably No. 7374, a 1948 Hawksworth Brake Compo, one of three converted for slip operation in 1958. No. 7374 was made at Bicester on 9 September 1960 and was used for the world's very last slip operation.

25.8.60 Michael Mensing

Class 165/0 Network Turbo 165039 at Bicester North with the 13.30 Birmingham Snow Hill to Marylebone train.

21.4.95 Author

Ardley, view down. This photograph was taken just prior to the opening of the station.

1910 Lens of Sutton

South portal of Ardley Tunnel. The radio aerial is on the left of the top of the arch, while in the centre of the wall is a stone bearing the date 1908.

21.4.95 Author

The twenty-four brick arches, each of 40 ft span, form Soulden No. 2 Viaduct.

1910 Author's collection

Banbury, Merton Street to Farthinghoe

The branch from Banbury to Verney Junction had 1 mile of track in Oxfordshire. In 1846 the Buckingham & Brackley Junction Railway was authorized to build a line from Winslow (Verney Junction) on the Oxford & Bletchley Junction Railway to Banbury. On 22 July 1847, these two companies amalgamated to become the Buckinghamshire Railway. Sir Harry Verney of Claydon, near Buckingham, and the Marquess of Chandos of Buckingham and Wotton had promoted both companies. Worked by the LNWR, the Buckinghamshire Railway opened to Banbury for passenger traffic on 1 May 1850 and to goods traffic on the 15th of the same month. The LNWR absorbed the company by an Act of 21 July 1879.

Meanwhile, on 9 July 1847 the Northampton & Banbury Railway Act was passed to build a line from Northampton through Towcester to Cockley Brake Junction, 5½ miles from Banbury and situated between Farthinghoe and Brackley stations. Although the LNWR agreed to build the line and lease it, time ran out before the railway was constructed. On 28 July 1863 a new Act was passed and the name of the company changed to the Northampton & Banbury Junction Railway (NBJR). Its eastern terminus was to be at Blisworth, as the LNWR had already built a line from Northampton to Blisworth over which the NBJR was granted running powers, in addition to those from Cockley Brake Junction to Banbury.

The NBJR had expansionist ideas, and in the mid-1860s it secured Acts for extending from Banbury to Chipping Norton and Ross, with running powers over the Ross & Monmouth line; over the Worcester, Dean Forest & Monmouth Railway; and over the Midland Railway (MR) from Beckford to Tewkesbury. To fit these grandiose ideas it changed its name to the Midland Counties & South Wales Railway. By 1870 it realized that these schemes would never come to fruition and its title reverted to the NBJR.

Meanwhile, the NBJR opened to Towcester on 1 May 1866 and, following the expiry of the 1863 powers, it secured an Act in 1870 that revived powers to build to Banbury. In fact, access to the town was over the Buckinghamshire Railway from Cockley Brake Junction. It opened on 1 June 1872. That year the NBJR stopped hiring locomotives from the LNWR and worked its line with engines purchased secondhand from that company, but the NBJR had too small a stud and the LNWR supplied engines from 1 March 1875.

The NBJR used rather primitive equipment. Signals were worked from ground frames; all points were hand-operated; and the levers had to be held when trains passed over the points.

On 1 July 1910 the Stratford-upon-Avon & Midland Junction Railway (SMJR) took over the NBJR. Passenger trains between Blisworth and Banbury were withdrawn on 2 July 1951 and the Towcester to Cockley Brake Junction line was closed four months later on 29 October. Despite the introduction of diesel railcars on the Buckingham line, which increased traffic by over 400 per cent and with a third reduction in running costs, the line still failed to pay its way and made an annual deficit of £14,000. The passenger service was withdrawn between Banbury, Merton Street station and Buckingham on 2 January 1961, and on 2 December 1963 the line from Banbury to Buckingham was closed and Merton Street yard was only accessible through Banbury General. Merton Street became a coal depot only from 4 May 1964 and was closed completely on 2 June 1966.

Banbury, Merton Street had a weatherboarded train shed. The front of the timber building remained largely unaltered, but in the late nineteenth century the simple two-sided platform was lengthened and the train shed roof of two gable sections was replaced with an arcaded roof supported on steel posts and tensioned with tie rods. In about 1956 the station was repainted and the train shed roof was removed, leaving just the framework and the timber walls. 'Banbury' appeared in large letters on a nameboard above the booking office. Turntables connected passenger platform roads with the goods shed. The LNWR station was parallel with that of the nearby GWR station and an exchange siding was provided.

The wooden goods shed was alongside the LNWR passenger station. On the opposite side to the passenger station was a cattle market, which provided the branch with considerable traffic. The goods yard had the usual coal wharves, and towards the station throat a siding led to the gas works. The original gas works was sited conveniently to receive coal via the Oxford Canal, but with the development of the railways, in 1854–6 it was repositioned between the LNWR and the GWR. Despite the proximity of rails, initially the transfer of coal to the retort house was by road and the by-products were loaded into barrels and taken by cart to the stations. The private siding was eventually laid in 1866, with access from both the LNWR and the GWR. Coal was delivered twice weekly, wagons being winched along the siding while the locomotive passed through the normal exchange siding between the two railways and collected empty wagons from the other side of the gas works.

Early in 1916, a mile along the branch from Banbury, a private siding was laid to the Ministry of Munitions shell-filling factory, the junction being close to Butcher's Crossing footpath across the line. After a train had entered the sidings and been locked in, its guard had to walk 1 mile to Banbury signal-box with the single line electric train staff so that other trains could use the section. In due course, after shunting operations were complete, he had to retrace his steps to Banbury to collect this staff, which gave him authority to leave the sidings.

Empty shell cases arrived by rail and loaded ones were despatched by the same means. All types of shell used by the Royal Artillery were filled, including those containing chlorine and mustard gas, anti-aircraft shells, mortar bombs, shrapnel shells and naval mines. Two 0–8–0s hauled the heavy loaded trains from the exchange sidings, facing a rise of 1 in 122.

Behind the seven exchange sidings was a complex of internal lines, including one crossing Overthorpe Road, the whole stretching for 1 mile. Shunting within the factory was carried out by *John*, Hudswell Clarke 0–6–0ST No. 327, which was built in 1889, and by *Lidban*, Avonside 0–6–0ST No. 1770, built in 1917. They were each fitted with electric lights, which were safer than oil lamps in the vicinity of explosives, and their chimneys carried spark arresting cowls. *John* was later used by Nott, Brodie & Co. Ltd on the Portway road contract between Bristol and Avonmouth, while *Lidban* was sold to Brymbo Steel Co. Ltd, Denbighshire. The filling factory closed in 1919, but until 1924 it was used by George Cohen Sons & Co. Ltd for the disposal of surplus high explosive. The site was then cleaned and returned to agricultural use.

The exterior of Banbury Merton Street station.

c. 1956 Lens of Sutton

In 1872–3 the NBJR purchased two 0–6–0s from the LNWR at £700 each and a 2–4–0T for £1000. The latter was interesting as it was one of the earliest side tanks, contemporary tanks usually being of the well or saddle variety. When the LNWR took over in 1875 the 0–6–0s were scrapped, but the 2–4–0T was sold for £800 to the Severn & Wye Railway & Canal Company, which named it *Ranger*. Converted to an 0–6–0ST in 1891, four years later it became GWR No. 1358 and was finally withdrawn in October 1896.

Locomotives appearing at Banbury, Merton Road, included 2–2–2s of the 'Problem' and 'Lady of the Lake' classes; 0–6–0s of the DX type, 'Coal Engines' and 'Cauliflowers' that worked passenger as well as goods trains; 0–8–0s of the G1, G2 and Super D classes; and 0–6–2Ts. In London, Midland & Scottish (LMS) days, six ex-Lancashire & Yorkshire Railway 0–6–0s appeared as well as MR/LMS 0–6–0s. Stanier and BR Standard 2–6–4Ts worked the passenger service from Bletchley, while a 0–6–0 and single coach handled passengers from Towcester. The Bletchley branch could not be economically worked by steam, and under the 1955 Modernisation Plan single-unit diesel railcars were ordered. Eight DMU workings started on 13 August 1956, working from Bletchley to Banbury using two specially adapted Derby lightweight cars, No. M79900 and No. M79901. None of the other lightweight cars were single units. The intention was that each railcar would work on alternate days, but it was found that on Thursdays (market day) and Saturdays a single car became so crowded that both had to be run. The luggage compartment was cramped due to the second driving cab having to be made. No. M79900 had a small luggage compartment and seats for sixty-one passengers. No. M79901 had a larger luggage compartment and seats for fifty-two passengers. In operation, the luggage accommodation of No. M79900 was found to be too small, and an extra nine seats had to be taken out and the partition moved. In June 1957 an additional late Saturday evening working was introduced to enable cinema goers to patronize films shown in Banbury.

The locomotive shed at Banbury, which was built of timber, opened in May 1851. The three-road shed held six engines. The turntable, originally by the passenger station, was replaced in 1917 by one installed south of the engine shed. This came secondhand from Bletchley. Following the First World War only one engine was stabled at Banbury. The shed closed on 11 April 1932, but the turntable remained in use until about October 1956.

Passenger services on the Buckingham line varied little in frequency over the years, being five each way daily. At first there was one each way on Sundays, but this number had doubled by 1922. The year 1952 saw a reduction to three trains each way daily. Until the First World War a slip-coach was detached from the 4.05 p.m. Euston, 5.01 p.m. Bletchley, arriving at Banbury at 6.32 p.m. and competing quite well with GWR timings.

The Banbury to Blisworth service in 1887 showed two to, and three from, Banbury, plus one each way on Thursdays. In 1910 there were three each way daily plus one each way on Thursdays. By 1922 the service had diminished to two each way and no extra train on Thursdays. This service lasted until its withdrawal in 1951.

In 1952 only one daily goods ran over the branch from Towcester. This was a pick-up goods train, generally hauled by a Class 3F 0–6–0 from Stratford-on-Avon shed. On Thursdays a cattle special ran from Banbury market. This was usually worked by a Class 4F 0–6–0 from Coalville, Crewe South, Nottingham, Northampton or Peterborough.

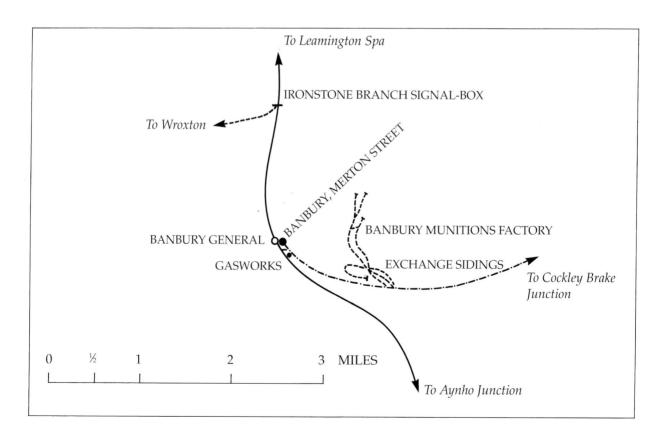

Ex-LMS 0–6–0 with one coach passenger train at Banbury Merton Street station. Notice the platform in the foreground, which consists of timber planking.

c. 1950 M.E.J. Deane

A 2–6–4T at Banbury Merton Street station with a passenger train.

c. 1950 Lens of Sutton

Banbury Merton Street station following the removal of most of the roof from the train shed. The single car DMU hardly requires a platform of this length. A plentiful supply of cattle wagons is stabled on the right.

c. 1956 Lens of Sutton

A two-car Derby-built DMU for Buckingham stands at Banbury Merton Street station. A GWR brake van is on the left.

1959 David Lawrence

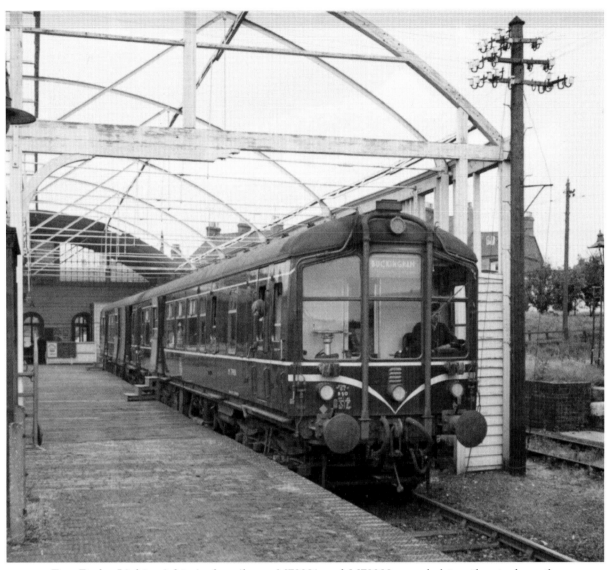

Two Derby Lightweight single railcars, M79901 and M79900, coupled together to form the 3.45 p.m. service to Buckingham.

6.8.60 Michael Mensing

Derby Lightweight single car M79900 arriving at Banbury Merton Street station with the 12.30 p.m. ex-Bletchley service. The buffer stops on the right are constructed solely of timber. A gasholder can be seen in the background on the right.

25.8.60 Michael Mensing

Details of the ticket barrier and an old nameboard. Notice the gas lamps.

c. 1956 Lens of Sutton

Wroxton Quarry Railway

On 1 January 1917, Baldwins Ltd and the Brymbo Steel Co. Ltd jointly leased mineral rights of land to the north and east of Wroxton. This was followed by land to the north-west the next year. Later in 1917, Stewarts & Lloyds Ltd, Baldwins and Brymbo formed the Oxfordshire Ironstone Co. Ltd. Although winning the ore was relatively simple because it was close to the surface, taking it to the GWR's main Banbury–Leamington Spa line was difficult, since Wroxton was 200 ft above it and the intervening valleys lay at right angles across the direct distance of 3½ miles. The Ministry of Munitions paid for the line. In mid-May 1917, Topham, Jones & Railton Ltd were appointed contractors. In addition to British workers, 250 German prisoners of war were used on the project. The contractors had five Manning Wardle locomotives, four steam navvies and almost a hundred tipping wagons.

Ore production began in January 1919, and output for the year was 81,346 tons. This was improved to 600,000 tons by 1929, but demand was far from constant. Production during the Second World War was at a high level and nearly 1¾ million tons were raised in 1956, the year of maximum output. Mining consisted of removing the shallow overburden, extracting the ironstone and then returning the ground to cultivation.

The railway had many features of a main line: signal-boxes at the principal level-crossings, with a wheel for opening the gates; signals; railside telephone posts; ¼ mile posts; and gradient posts.

The single-track main line from Pinhill Farm to Wroxton was doubled in 1953 to cope with increasing traffic. Trains used the right-hand track as the crusher was on the south side of the line and normal left-hand working would have involved crossing the Up line.

On each working day, about six trips were made from the GWR exchange sidings to Wroxton with fourteen empty hoppers, returning with the same number of loaded wagons. The journey time was approximately 20–25 minutes for the distance of 4½ miles. The locomotive propelled a train to Wroxton and always faced uphill to ensure that the firebox crown was always covered. From April 1963, when six ex-GWR brake vans were purchased, trains were hauled to Wroxton. When BR advised that four vacuum brake-fitted wagons per train plus a brake van would allow longer trains to be worked safely, five of the six-wheeled engines were fitted with vacuum brakes.

An output of 40,000 tons per week at the end of 1965 decreased dramatically to 2,000 tons eighteen months later, a two-day week having to be worked. An economy was made in the spring of 1967 when some of the line was singled, nevertheless the situation was such that the line closed on 30 September 1967 and the track was lifted the following year.

The Oxfordshire Ironstone Railway (OIR) formed a junction with the GWR Down goods loop at Ironstone Mines signal-box (renamed Ironstone Branch signal-box in 1958), 3 miles north of Banbury. Four terminal wagon storage sidings and six exchange sidings

Hudswell Clarke 0–4–0ST *Betty* pushing a train of loaded ore wagons. Notice the draught shield for the cab and also the centre coupler, utilized on internal use wagons.

20.5.63 Revd Alan Newman

were provided. In 1939 a siding was made to the Northern Aluminium Co.'s works. In 1940, Northern Aluminium purchased an 0–4–0ST built by Peckett in 1917, and in 1948 it replaced it with a new F.C. Hibberd & Co. Ltd four-wheel diesel-mechanical locomotive. This was sold in April 1965 and, until closure in about 1968, shunting was performed by an Oxfordshire Ironstone Co. locomotive.

At Pinhill Farm, 1 mile from the junction with the GWR, were the original headquarters of the OIR, with a two-road, corrugated iron locomotive shed holding four engines. A brick-built workshop and two calcining kilns were alongside. In 1929 the engine shed was extended to hold six, and an additional corrugated iron shed to hold two more engines was built in 1938. The line continued on a ruling gradient of 1 in 54. Beyond Moor Hill Crossing, south-east of Horley, trains encountered a rise of 1 in 35, the steepest on the line. At Wroxton, branches led to various quarries, some up to 2 miles distant.

In the mid-1930s a long, single-road engine shed capable of holding five locomotives was opened at Wroxton. An extra shed, built in 1953, was doubled four years later when the average allocation there was nine. A locomotive repair shop was erected at Wroxton in 1958.

In 1923 there was a stud of six engines, and between 1924 and 1935 the number fluctuated between seven and nine. The penultimate steam locomotive, *Phyllis*, a four-wheel vertical boiler 200 hp Sentinel purchased in 1956, was not a success. Thirty steam locomotives worked the line at various times. Their livery of crimson lake was kept very clean. All were scrapped except for No. 1 *Sir Thomas*, which was preserved at Quainton Road.

The six-wheeled engines were based at Pinhill Farm shed for working the main line while the 0–4–0STs worked between the quarries and the crusher, and were stabled at Wroxton. The six-wheelers were given boys' names and the four-wheelers girls' names. From 1936, engines had names only, but the others had numbers as well. The engines were fitted with combination couplings: buckeye for coupling to dump cars taking stone to the crushers; link for GWR/BR wagons.

The Sentinel 0–4–0 diesel-hydraulic *Grace* arrived in 1961, followed by twelve similar machines. Diesels for quarry working weighed 30/31 tons and those for the main line weighed 40 tons. Quarry engines had a lower gearbox ratio. These continued to be named after girls, and those of the main line after boys. The four-wheel dump cars had relatively shallow bodies, centrally pivoted and arranged so that they could be side-tipped in either direction. They had automatic couplings of the buckeye type.

A workmen's train ran from Pinhill Farm to Wroxton in the morning and returned them after they had finished work. For most of the life of the railway, workmen travelled in an ex-North London Railway luggage van and then in a box van, but latterly they used an ex-GWR brake van.

Wroxton Quarries' steam locomotives:

Name	Wheel arrangement	Maker	Maker's no.	Date of building
No. 1 *Sir Thomas*	0–6–0T	Hudswell Clarke	1334	1918
No. 2 *Lord North*	0–6–0T	Hudswell Clarke	1346	1918
No. 6 *Frodsham*	0–6–0ST	Manning Wardle	1013	1887
No. 8 *Gowy*	0–6–0ST	Manning Wardle	1119	1889
No. 14	0–6–0ST	Manning Wardle	1749	1909
Nancy	0–6–0ST	Hunslet	356	1885
Ironstone	0–4–0ST	Hunslet	344	1885
No. 3 *The President*	0–6–0ST	Hudswell Clarke	1419	1923
Noel	0–4–0ST	Peckett	1172	1912
Phyllis	0–4–0ST	Bagnall	1453	1895
No. 4 *The Dean*	0–6–0ST	Hunslet	1496	1926
No. 5 *Treasurer*	0–6–0ST	Hunslet	1446	1929
No. 5 *Basic*	0–6–0ST	Peckett	1867	1935
No. 6 *Gwen*	0–4–0ST	Hudswell Clarke	1662	1936
Grace	0–4–0ST	Peckett	1894	1936
Maud	0–4–0ST	Peckett	1937	1938
Sir Charles	0–6–0ST	Peckett	1943	1938
The Bursar	0–6–0ST	Hunslet	1645	1930
John (*Joan* till 1957)	0–6–0ST	Peckett	1981	1940
Allan	0–6–0ST	Peckett	1997	1941
Spencer	0–6–0ST	Hunslet	2374	1941
Graham (*Hellidon* till 1953)	0–6–0ST	Hunslet	2415	1941
No. 2 *Byfield*	0–6–0ST	Bagnall	2655	1942
Mary	0–4–0ST	Hudswell Clarke	1818	1950
Newlay	0–4–0ST	Hunslet	1292	1917
Barnsley	0–4–0ST	Hudswell Clarke	727	1905
Alex	0–6–0ST	Hunslet	3716	1952
Barabel	0–4–0ST	Hudswell Clarke	1868	1953
Betty	0–4–0ST	Hudswell Clarke	1869	1953
Phyllis	4wVBT	Sentinel	9615	1956
303. No. 2 *Joan*	0–4–0ST	Avonside	1822	1919
Jean (*Betty* till 1958)	0–4–0ST	Hudswell Clarke	1696	1939
Frank	0–6–0ST	Hunslet	3872	1958

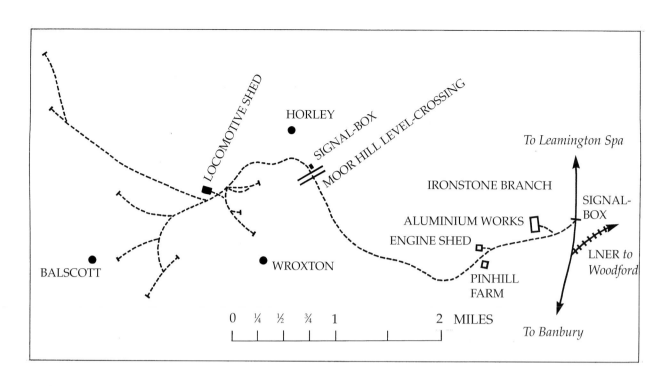

Phyllis, a four-wheel vertical boiler Sentinel, built in 1956.

23.3.65 Revd Alan Newman

The Dean, a Hunslet 0–6–0ST, and ex-LNER van forming a workmen's train. A wooden bench is inside the open door.

15.9.56 Hugh Davies

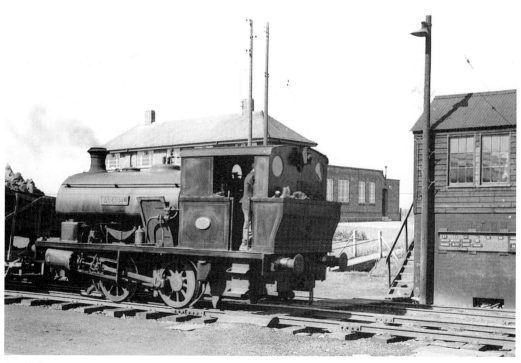

Barabel, a Hudswell Clarke 0–4–0ST, passing Wroxton signal-box, which has a roster board fixed to its outside wall.

13.4.57 Hugh Davies

Barabel with a train being loaded with ore.

17.7.64 Revd Alan Newman

Hunslet 0–6–0ST *Spencer*, built in 1941.

4.10.60 Revd Alan Newman

Peckett 0–6–0ST *Basic*, built in 1935.

4.10.60 Revd Alan Newman

Grace, a Sentinel four-wheel diesel-hydraulic, built in 1961.

23.3.65 Revd Alan Newman

Frank, a Hunslet 0–6–0ST, working empty tippler wagons near Drayton. Note the ex-GWR brake van at the rear.

11.5.64 Michael Mensing

Kingham to King's Sutton

The Kingham to King's Sutton branch linking two main lines was built in two sections. The first to be built under an Act of 31 July 1854 was from Chipping Norton Junction, as Kingham was then called, to Chipping Norton. It was built under the aegis of the Oxford, Worcester & Wolverhampton Railway (OWWR), nicknamed from its initials 'The Old Worse & Worse'. William Bliss, a tweed manufacturer of Chipping Norton, was the prime mover for a railway to the town as he needed one to bring coal to power his mill and take away the finished product.

The contractors responsible for building the line were Peto & Betts, Sir Samuel Morton Peto himself subscribing over half of the sum required. Landowners were generous, resulting in the line being built for only £6,000 a mile, a great improvement over the more usual figure of £12,000. It is interesting to record that some of the wagons Peto used on this contract found their way to the Balaclava Railway, a military line constructed by Peto during the Crimean War. He refused to take remuneration for building this Russian railway thus earning himself a baronetcy in 1854. Peto was an excellent contractor, and his four hundred navvies working day and night had the 4½ miles of line opened on 10 August 1855, less than a year after the commencement of works.

A celebratory dinner was held at the Town Hall, Chipping Norton, presided over by the mayor, the mayors of Banbury and Stratford-upon-Avon being among the guests. The town was in holiday mood, with shops closed, church bells ringing and a brass band playing.

As with many small railways, it did not purchase its own locomotives and rolling-stock, but found it more economic to be worked by a larger company, in this case the OWWR. It was worked for half of the gross receipts, the OWWR eventually purchasing the line in 1859, guaranteeing a dividend of 4 per cent. In due course the OWWR became part of the West Midland Railway, which was taken over by the GWR on 1 August 1863. Meanwhile a branch was opened southwards from Kingham to Bourton-on-the-Water on 1 March 1862. (For more details of this line see *Branch Lines of Gloucestershire*.)

For a railway to be really profitable, it needed to be part of a through route. The two branches from Kingham called out for an extension northwards to Banbury and southwards to Cheltenham. To this end the Banbury & Cheltenham Railway Act was passed on 21 July 1873. In November 1874, Edward Wilson, engineer to the new line, was allowed to start active work on it. Great things were expected. Beside the line between Hook Norton and King's Sutton was found brown haematite capable of yielding up to as much as 27 per cent of metallic ore, and it was confidently expected that this ironstone would provide the line's stable traffic. Estimate suggested that one Welsh firm would require 1,000 tons daily, while the total daily tonnage would amount to 10,000 tons – in other words, a thousand wagon loads, or at least twenty trains. In view of this anticipated traffic, loops of 800 ft in length were laid on the single line so that trains could pass. Promoters also advanced other advantages, such as improved access to South Wales coal; cattle being more easily transported to Banbury market; and a more convenient route for timber from Gloucester to Banbury. Shareholders became a little apprehensive when the financial crisis of 1878 caused work to be suspended for over a year. When the contractor resumed, priority was given to the Cheltenham to Bourton section as all of the stations, apart from Notgrove, were complete and three-quarters of the route had been laid with track, whereas only about 9 miles of the eastern section from Chipping Norton to King's Sutton were ready. The Cheltenham to Bourton stretch was opened in 1881 and that from King's Sutton to Chipping Norton on 6 April 1887. A new through station was built at Chipping Norton to replace the old terminus. On 1 July 1897 the Banbury & Cheltenham Direct Railway was bought by the GWR for £138,000.

So that through trains could cross the main Oxford to Worcester line at Kingham without interfering with trains on that line, a flyover was built under the GWR (Additional Powers) Act of 4 August 1905. It was opened on 8 January 1906, ready for the Ports to Ports Express which used the Banbury & Cheltenham Direct Railway from May 1906 until September 1939.

After the Second World War, traffic on the line fell into decline. The Chipping Norton to Banbury passenger service was withdrawn on 4 June 1951, and the once heavy ironstone traffic had decreased to such an extent that only one goods train ran, as opposed to the former sixteen daily ironstone trains. The line between Great Rollright Siding and Hook Norton was shut by a landslip in August 1959, Kingham to Chipping Norton was closed to passengers on 3 December 1962, Hook Norton to Adderbury closed completely on 4 November 1963 and Adderbury to King's Sutton was closed on 5 April 1970.

Kingham station opened on 10 August 1855 as Chipping Norton Junction, and it was renamed Kingham in about 1914. At first only a two-platform station, a bay was added for the opening of the branch to Chipping Norton. In about 1906 a second branch platform was built. The station had several interesting features, one being that at one time it had four signal-boxes – North, South, East and West – a nomenclature probably unique on the GWR. Also, the Down home signals on the platform were hung from a bracket so that they could be seen below a bridge. The third feature was that the nearby Langston Arms inn had an entrance from the station footbridge. Following the closure of the branches, Kingham reverted to a two-road station.

Leaving No. 4 platform, a train curved to the north-east and at Kingham East Junction joined the direct line from Cheltenham. One track of this flyover closed on 23 September 1953, its original purpose of carrying the Ports to Ports Express and mineral trains over the main line having ceased. One road was retained to form a triangle with the Chipping Norton and Bourton-on-the-Water branches for engine turning purposes. The line was eventually taken out of use in 1960 and then lifted in November 1961.

Sarsden Halt, with a timber platform and corrugated iron pagoda, opened on 2 July 1906 and, unusually, boasted a siding. The signal-box was not a block post. The crossing keeper/porter worked the gates and the two distant signals, but to release the point levers the train staff had to be inserted into the frame. The nearest village was Churchill, and it was the landowner, J.H. Langstone, who lived at Sarsden House beyond Churchill who requested that it should be named after his house.

Approaching Chipping Norton, a siding from the gas works trailed in. The station had a fairly large yard with six sidings, one of which served the spacious goods shed and another the cattle pens. A trailing siding ran to William Bliss's tweed mill, which produced army and horse clothing, shawls, railway rugs and tweed cloth. This was a sizeable enterprise, and Bliss's employees numbered about seven hundred.

The first station closed on 6 April 1887, a new through station being opened when the line was extended through to King's Sutton. This replacement had dual height fencing consisting of vertical posts with three triangular section arris rails making longitudinal battens. Each panel of sixteen palings had half-height palings used alternately with those of standard height. The site of the original station was used for the new standard goods shed with glazed end gables. Chipping Norton closed to goods traffic on 7 September 1964. Beyond the station was Chipping Norton Tunnel, which was 685 yd in length.

Great Rollright was originally only served by a siding, but on 12 December 1906 the GWR opened a halt that, in addition to local passengers, was intended to encourage tourist traffic to the sixty-five Rollright stones. Just beyond the siding the branch reached its summit 600 ft above sea level, before the descent of 11 miles.

The line passed through the 418 yd long Hook Norton Tunnel, and beyond was a trailing siding to the Earl of Dudley's ironstone quarries. As these were on the valley floor, their output had to be conveyed by cable-worked incline up to the siding. The quarries were opened in about 1901 and closed in April 1916.

The line crossed No. 2 and No. 1 viaducts, which were 296 and 188 yd in length respectively and both 90 ft high. Their construction took four hundred men four years, while after their closure four men with acetylene torches took only four weeks to demolish them. No. 2 had eight spans and No. 1, five. These viaducts were not built without loss of life. On 3 December 1885, Charles Hicks and Edward Gaskins were working on the timber supports near the top of a viaduct pier when the timber gave way and they fell 65 ft to their deaths.

Hook Norton station and goods shed were both built of brick. The goods shed office, and the others on the branch, were unusual in having two storeys. Hook Norton, Bloxham and Adderbury stations were all similar and had a central recessed wall area on the platform side, roof ridges of two levels and curved end valences to the canopy. From the goods siding at Hook Norton a line connected with Hook Norton Ironstone Partnership Ltd's quarry. Opened in about 1890, the quarry closed in 1901 when the company ran into financial difficulties. The GWR, as principal creditor, took its Manning Wardle tank engine, *Hook Norton*, which was built in 1889. As a complete contrast to its duties to date, it spent most of the remainder of its life handling boat trains along Weymouth Quay.

Just over ½ mile beyond Hook Norton was Council Hill Siding, which made a trailing connection with the Brymbo Steel Co. Ltd's ironstone quarries. A notable feature there was the four tall calcining kilns, where 2 ft gauge wagons were lifted to the top and the ore was tipped into the kiln for refining by burning. From chutes at the foot of each kiln the calcined ore was discharged into standard gauge wagons. Working started in December 1899 and ceased in June 1946.

Bloxham station, similar to that at Hook Norton, also closed to goods on 4 November 1963. At one time the village had its own gas works. After the Second World War, hundreds of wagon loads of prefabricated houses were stored at Barford airfield awaiting distribution. By the cattle pen, a private siding branched to the Northamptonshire Ironstone Co. Ltd's working, which was opened in 1918 to cope with the wartime demand. It was worked by Peckett-built 0–6–0ST *Northfield* and later by a four-wheeled petrol-electric – a rebuild of a 60 cm gauge engine made in 1917 by Nasmyth Wilson for the War Department. The quarry closed temporarily on 28 February 1942 and reopened early in 1948. It proved uneconomic and closed finally on 15 May 1954.

Beyond the station were Bloxham Ironstone Co. Ltd's sidings, which were opened in February 1918. The ore was loaded directly into standard gauge wagons. Between April 1918 and May 1919 the quarry employed thirty German prisoners of war from Banbury Camp. At various times the line used four 0–6–0STs, named *Barry, Betty, Edgar* and *Margôt* – the latter probably the only British locomotive nameplate to carry a circumflex. The post-war drop in demand caused temporary closure in 1921. The line was reopened, but the last ore was removed in June 1927. Beyond the exchange sidings was Milton Halt, set high on an embankment. Opened on 1 January 1908, it had a single wooden platform with a pagoda shelter.

Adderbury station was similar to Bloxham and, like Bloxham, the village had its own gas works. The yard had a private siding serving an ironstone quarry, whose only locomotives were for a 1 ft 8 in gauge line. The quarry closed in about 1939 and in 1940 the site was used by Northern Aluminium Co. (Alcan). Railway wagons brought wrecked British and German aircraft, and there they were melted into ingots, which were taken out by road. In post-war years the site was used by the Twyford Seed Factory. On 1 August 1906 the line to King's Sutton was doubled, but it was singled again on 12 December 1965. Adderbury closed to goods on 4 December 1967.

Just 1 mile beyond Adderbury were Sydenham Sidings. Alfred Hickman Ltd opened an ironstone quarry in March 1914. Narrow gauge wagons took ore to the top of the calcining kilns, which after processing was discharged into standard gauge wagons. The quarry closed in June 1925.

Beyond this site the line crossed the 43 yd long River Cherwell Viaduct across the Oxford Canal and the River Cherwell. A shorter viaduct of flood arches was beyond. This curved stretch of line was used for overnight stops of the royal train when it was in the Banbury area. A locomotive always remained coupled to it to provide steam heating.

The branch trailed into the Oxford to Banbury line at King's Sutton in Northamptonshire, the River Cherwell marking the county boundary. King's Sutton was a two-platformed station, and no bay was provided as branch passenger trains worked through to and from Banbury.

The Kingham to Chipping Norton line was first worked by two small tank engines, which were built by George Stephenson's son, Robert, in 1859. An outstanding feature was their large American-type cab, very unusual at a time when British locomotives were either cabless or had just a primitive shelter. No. 52 was name *Ben Jonson*, and its nameless sister, No. 53, was affectionately known to the staff as 'Mrs Jonson'. Both were withdrawn from working branch trains in February 1877. Subsequently, passenger services were worked by 517 and 48XX class 0–4–2Ts, 'Metro' class 2–4–0Ts and steam railcars. Ore trains were worked by 26XX 2–6–0s and 28XX 2–8–0s, while 0–6–0s worked local trains. Class 43XX 2–6–0s were employed for duties ranging from the Ports to Ports Express to local pick-up goods. In addition, a variety of 4–4–0 'Bulldogs' worked this express in their day, as did 4–6–0 'Manors', the largest passenger engines allowed on the branch. Latterly, 41XX 2–6–2Ts worked Kingham to Chipping Norton passenger services.

The engine shed at Kingham opened in 1881 and had timber walls with a water tank forming the roof. It closed in 1906. The 22 ft diameter turntable was replaced by one of 45 ft diameter in March 1904. A new brick-built shed opened in 1913 and was closed in December 1962.

The stone-built shed at Chipping Norton opened in August 1855. The timber coaling platform was beneath the water tank. Between the tank and six supporting columns, with raised capitals from which sprang small brackets to give support to the tank, was a narrow cast-iron beam, which was pierced and visually very attractive. A water crane was attached to the underside of the tank. The shed closed in July 1922. It was to have been converted to a stationmaster's house, but in 1929 it was being used as garage accommodation.

With the opening of the Chipping Norton branch, three trains ran in each direction daily, the fares being 10*d* first class and 9*d* second. With the opening through to King's Sutton, four trains ran each way daily taking 55 minutes for the distance of 20 miles. No trains ran on Sundays. By 1910 the frequency increased to six each way and by 1922 there were additionally five railmotors from Kingham to King's Sutton. Bloxham, Milton and Adderbury were within 4 miles of Banbury by road, but 9, 7 and 6 miles respectively by rail. Rail travel was more expensive – Bloxham to Banbury was 1*s* 4*d* by train and 9*d* by bus.

Initially the Ports to Ports Express, when inaugurated in May 1906, ran from Newcastle-on-Tyne to Barry, but in later years two further ports were linked with the service by running a through coach to and from Hull via Goole. The Ports to Ports Express usually consisted of six coaches, including a restaurant car, LNER and GWR stock being used on alternate days. After fast running on the LNER, passengers must have found the 82 minutes allowed for the 44¾ miles from Banbury to Cheltenham rather an anticlimax. The express reappeared after the Second World War but in a modified form, running between Banbury and Newport over the much longer route via Oxford, Swindon and the Severn Tunnel, instead of over the Banbury & Cheltenham line.

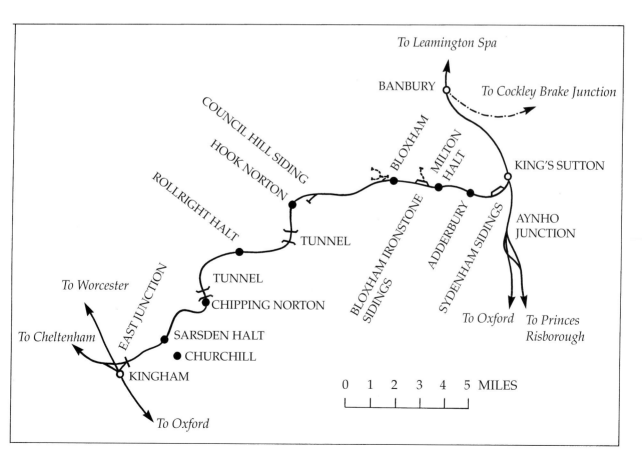

Kingham, with its original name of Chipping Norton Junction, view Down. A workman is carrying out repair to the roof of the footbridge. Milk churns stand near the foot of the stairs. The 517 class 0–4–2T, centre right, may have worked from King's Sutton.

c. 1905 Lens of Sutton

A 517 class 0–4–2T, No. 835, at Kingham after arriving from Chipping Norton. Trailer No. 115 has recently been converted from steam railmotor No. 19.

30.8.19 Author's collection

Kingham engine shed and turntable. The pillar with twin handles was used for turning an engine. On the left is the flyover bridge.

c. 1913 Author's collection

Down signals at Kingham, slung low so as to be visible below the footbridge. In the background, from left to right, are the flyover; Kingham North signal-box; an engine shed (to close in December 1962) and a water-tower.

17.8.62 Author

A 28XX class 2–8–0, No. 2887, passing Kingham North signal-box with an Up goods train. The flyover is in the background.

17.8.62 Author

A 5101 class 2–6–2T, No. 4100, arriving at Kingham with the 2.50 p.m. train from Cheltenham, signalled into one of the Chipping Norton branch platforms. The coaches are brake compo W6543W and brake third W1783W.

17.8.62 Author

A 5101 class 2–6–2T, No. 4142, leaving Kingham with the 4.00 p.m. service to Chipping Norton.
2.9.61 Michael Mensing

A 5101 class 2–6–2T, No. 5154, leaving Kingham with the 4.00 p.m. train to Chipping Norton.
31.8.62 Michael Mensing

The site of the former Kingham East Junction. The flyover line, curving right, was taken out of use on 23 September 1953, except for engine turning, and the track was removed in November 1961.
17.8.62 Author

A 5101 class 2–6–2T, No. 4100, near Kingham with the 4.53 p.m. train from Chipping Norton. The engine does not display a headlamp.

17.8.62 Author

A 517 class 0–4–2T arriving at Sarsden Halt with a train to Chipping Norton. Notice the railwayman's allotment, on the right and the battens on the ramp allowing the feet to purchase.

c. 1910 Author's collection

Sarsden signal-box and siding, view east.

17.8.62 Author

A 517 class 0–4–2T at Chipping Norton with a two-coach train for Kingham. The fencing is of standard and half-height palings.

c. 1905 Lens of Sutton

Chipping Norton, view towards Kingham. The open cab engine has polished dome and safety valve casing. The lime shows on the floor of the two cattle wagons. A traction engine is at work in the goods yard. The goods shed and office are on the far right.

c. 1910 Paul Strong collection

A 517 class 0–4–2T, No. 546, has set off for the main line before the protecting points were changed. The signal-box steps were probably destroyed, hence the ladder giving access to Chipping Norton West signal-box. The brake van bears a cast plate that read 'Wolverhampton' and a cast number, 56124.

c. 1910 Author's collection

A 5101 class 2–6–2T, No. 4101, with the 4.25 p.m. Saturdays-only train to Kingham. The platform canopy has now been removed.

4.10.62 Author's collection

A train of evacuees arrives at Chipping Norton. The children have rucksacks and gas masks. The train, of at least eleven coaches, is one of the longest ever to use the branch.

1.9.39 Lens of Sutton

A 55XX class 2–6–2T, No. 5538, at Chipping Norton with the 4.35 p.m. Saturdays-only service to Kingham. The engine's water tanks are being replenished. No. 5538 is now preserved at Steamtown, Carnforth.

2.4.55 Hugh Ballantyne

Chipping Norton Co-operative Society Limited's wagon No. 9. Painted black with white letters, it was built in February 1900.

February 1900 Author's collection

Rollright Halt. The six workmen with a pair of steps are painting the halt, probably prior to its opening on 12 December 1906. The postcard caption writer was inaccurate in putting 'Great'. The village is Great Rollright, but the halt is simply Rollright.

c. 1906 Lens of Sutton

Hook Norton station, view Up. Notice the sharp curves. Beyond the goods shed are low-sided wagons. The new signal-box was opened in 1907. The card if postmarked 23.8.15.

c. 1910 Paul Strong collection

A Cardiff to Newcastle express passes Hook Norton, the five coaches headed by an outside frame 4–4–0.

c. 1910 Lens of Sutton

A five-coach passenger train of four-wheel vehicles crossing Hook Norton Viaduct, probably hauled by a 517 class 0–4–2T. Kilns can be seen beyond the arch below the train. Beneath the viaduct is a ropeway connecting with the Earl of Dudley's iron ore workings.

c. 1905 Paul Strong collection

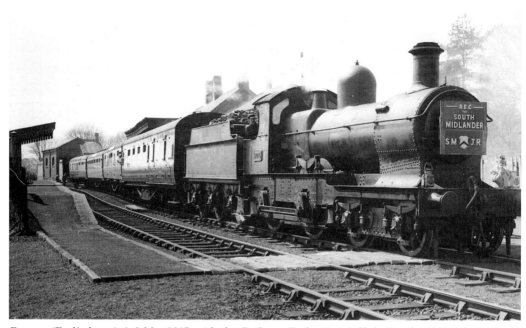

Former 'Earl' class 4–4–0 No. 9015 with the Railway Enthusiasts' Club 'South Midlander'. It had come from Kingham.

24.4.55 Hugh Ballantyne

No. 1337 *Hook Norton* at Weymouth. This Manning Wardle 0–6–0ST was acquired from Hook Norton Ironstone Partnership liquidators.

c. 1906 Author's collection

A 517 class 0–4–2T and autotrailer at Bloxham, working an Up train.

c. 1910 Lens of Sutton

Brymbo kilns, a tub hoist and tippers, Hook Norton.

c. 1910 Author's collection

Adderbury view Up. The line to the ironstone pits connected from the right behind the signal-box. Notice the profusion of oil lamps.

c. 1920 Lens of Sutton

A 43XX class 2–6–0, No. 5361, at Adderbury, working a Kingham to Banbury freight train. Oxford University Railway Society members were riding in the brake van.

28.2.59 P.Q. Treloar

King's Sutton, view Down. Constructed of brick with limestone dressings, the station has attractive chimneys. There is no bay or island platform, which is unusual for a junction station.

17.8.62 Author

A 4–4–0, No. 4112 *Oxford*, passes King's Sutton with an Up express train.

c. 1920 Author's collection

Kidlington to Blenheim & Woodstock

In 1885 the 8th Duke of Marlborough planned the Woodstock Railway to run from Shipton-on-Cherwell to Woodstock, the Act being passed on 25 September 1886. Most of the capital was placed either by the contractors, Lucas & Aird, or by their nominees. Construction began in March 1888 and it is believed that steam navvies were used for excavating the cuttings. Although the line was substantially completed early in 1889, the GWR was unwilling to permit branch trains to run over its main line to a junction at Shipton-on-Cherwell and desired the branch to run parallel with its Down line for 1 mile to Woodstock Road station. Lucas & Aird added the third line in the winter of 1889/90 and extended the Down platform at Woodstock Road by 300 ft, forming a bay road. Meanwhile, on 14 November 1889 the GWR agreed to work the branch when it was completed.

Col. Rich inspected the new line on 14 May 1890, his two-coach special being hauled by Lucas & Aird's Manning Wardle 0–6–0ST No. 132. The branch opened on 19 May 1890 when Woodstock Road station was renamed Kidlington. The usual celebrations took place and on its first day the line carried 7 first class, 7 second class and 418 third class passengers.

The Woodstock Railway proved economically unviable and the GWR purchased it for £15,000. It became part of the GWR on 1 July 1897. To its new owners the line proved a good investment, and in the early years of the century the GWR booked about 17,000 tickets annually at Woodstock and handled 8,504 tons of minerals and goods.

Daily average of wagons, 1925:

Coal & mineral		General goods		Churns of milk	Livestock trucks
Forward	Received	Forward	Received	per annum	per annum
–	3	2	3	2,336	96

From 1934 onwards the annual number of loads of livestock traffic over the branch was in single figures. Apart from general traffic and coal, Woodstock received bricks, stone, timber, and skins for the glove factory. Outward traffic included agricultural produce and gloves. In the early days up to two hundred cattle wagons had been dealt with annually.

Unlike many branches, the number of passengers using the line fell during the Second World War, the quantity of tickets issued at Woodstock being 19,500 in 1943 and 17,500 in 1945. The bus was so much more convenient, offering a direct service to the centre of Oxford thus avoiding a change at Kidlington and a walk from Oxford station. By 1952, ticket sales had declined to 9,000, each train carrying an average of five or six passengers. The result was that the branch closed entirely on 1 March 1954. On Saturday 27 February, 0–4–2T No. 1420, which is now preserved on the South Devon Railway, ran the last services.

Kidlington station, whose nameboards read 'Kidlington Change for Blenheim & Woodstock', was of Brunellian style architecture executed in Cotswold stone, passengers being protected by an all-round canopy. The broad gauge type goods shed was built of yellow brick. From the late 1890s the station garden was very attractive, trellis work being an unusual feature.

In 1923 the Oxfordshire Farmers' Bacon Factory opened adjacent to the station and was rail-connected at a cost of £850, refunded to the firm by a 5 per cent rebate on traffic for not more than 10 years. The business failed, but on 6 October 1930 it was purchased by Messrs C&T Harris (Calne) Ltd and traffic recommenced until the private siding agreement terminated on 8 December 1966.

In May 1942 the first ½ mile of the branch was converted into a goods loop by installing a power-worked point to enable trains to regain the Down main. The Government footed the cost of £3,460. North of Kidlington, branch trains crossed a two-span bridge over the River Cherwell, soon to recross it via another two-span bridge. Immediately beyond they curved north-west away from the main line, the branch crossing the Oxford Canal by yet another two-span bridge, a girder section crossing the waterway and towpath, and a brick arch over an adjacent bridleway. The branch climbed on a gradient of 1 in 92, steepening to 1 in 69 as it passed over the A423 on a steel girder bridge before descending to Shipton-on-Cherwell Halt. Built at a cost of £160 and opened 1 April 1929, the halt had a timber waiting shelter and rail-level platform. In 1933 a further £120 was spent providing a standard height timber platform.

The line climbed at 1 in 129 to Blenheim & Woodstock station. Built of limestone to a GWR standard design usually executed in brick, it had ashlar quoins and window surrounds. The lamp standards, atypical for the GWR, were of attractive barley sugar pattern, but carried a standard GWR harp-type suspension bracket. Unlike many branch stations, it was sited close to the town centre. It was also unusual in that in the station name the palace came first and the town second. In contrast with the passenger station, the goods shed was of corrugated iron. Another curiosity was the signal-box, which was unusually lofty so as to allow the signalman a clear view over the nearby water tank and engine shed. In 1928, sugar beet started to be sent from Woodstock to a new factory at Eynsham on the Witney branch, but unfortunately this traffic ceased when Eynsham works closed in 1931.

The first train on the Woodstock branch was worked by a 517 class 0–4–2T. In the mid-1890s, No. 1473 of the class, which was built in 1883, was specially named *Fair Rosamund*, for working the royal train which took the Prince of Wales over the branch on 23 November 1896. The train left Paddington at 4.55 p.m. and ran non-stop to Kidlington, where the main line engine was replaced by *Fair Rosamund*. It arrived at Woodstock at 6.39 p.m., 1 minute ahead of schedule. *Fair Rosamund* bore flags and a wreath with 'Welcome' in the centre. The name came from Rosamund de Clifford of Clifford Castle near Hay-on-Wye. Said to be the most beautiful woman of the period, she lived in a bower near Woodstock that was built by her lover, King Henry II. The bower was so cunningly constructed that none outside the secret could penetrate its mazy entrance, though Queen Eleanor of Aquitaine eventually found her way in and soon despatched her rival with poison. No. 1473 continued to work the branch for another forty years until its withdrawal in August 1935. It was most unusual for the GWR to name a tank engine.

CLOSURE OF RAILWAY LINE
BLENHEIM & WOODSTOCK BRANCH

The British Transport Commission hereby give notice that on and from Monday, 1st March, 1954 the passenger and freight train services over the above mentioned line will be discontinued. Blenheim & Woodstock Station and Shipton-on-Cherwell Halt will be closed.

Facilities for passengers are available at Handborough (for Blenheim & Woodstock) and at Kidlington or Bletchington (for Shipton-on-Cherwell). A new Omnibus service will be introduced by City of Oxford Motor Services Ltd. between Oxford and Woodstock via Kidlington and Shipton-on-Cherwell.

The existing services for collection and delivery of Passenger rated traffic will, with certain exceptions, be maintained from Handborough Station. Collection and delivery of Goods "smalls" traffic in the area hitherto served by the line will be continued.

Collection orders for Passengers' luggage in advance should be sent to or handed in at Handborough Station.

Merchandise traffic in full truck loads will be dealt with at Kidlington Bletchington, Heyford and Handborough Stations, according to traders' requirements.

Any further information in respect of the arrangements for dealing with traffic and any other matters arising out of the closing of the line will be supplied on application to the Station Masters at Kidlington, Bletchington Heyford or Handborough or from the following Officers :—

District Goods Superintendent, 14 Bath Road, Reading
(Tel. Reading 4281. Ext. 359)
in respect of merchandise traffic at Kidlington Bletchington and Heyford Stations.

District Operating Superintendent, Paddington
(Tel. Paddington 7000. Ext. 2259)
in respect of passenger and parcels traffic

District Commercial Superintendent, Worcester
(Tel. Worcester 3241. Ext. 47)
in respect of merchandise, passenger and parcels traffic at Handborough Station.

PADDINGTON STATION
January, 1954

K. W. C. GRAND
Chief Regional Manager

Notice of closure of the Blenheim & Woodstock branch, 1 March 1954.

'Metro' class 2–4–0Ts occasionally appeared, and in about 1907–8 some services were worked by steam railmotors. In August 1935, *Fair Rosamund* was replaced by 48XX class 0–4–2Ts. 54XX class 0–6–0PTs were popular for freight and shunting. In the summer of 1949 a GWR diesel railcar was diagrammed for afternoon workings. The 517 class was limited to trains of 140 tons and the 'Metro' and 48XX classes to trains of 168 tons. Trains were limited to 30 m.p.h.

The engine shed at Woodstock was of wrought iron framing clad with corrugated iron sheeting. When track alterations were made to lengthen the passenger platform in March 1899, the shed was shortened by 23 ft, resited, the Woodstock end blocked up and the shed approached from the Kidlington side. A survey carried out in 1925 concluded that savings could be made if the shed closed and the engine was transferred to Oxford. It also recommended that all trains should be push and pull operations so that run-round facilities could be abolished, thus effecting further savings. The shed closed on 17 June 1927 and was removed the following year.

An accident occurred on 8 November 1897 when the 3.15 p.m. from Woodstock collided with the buffers at Kidlington. The vacuum brake pipe had not been connected between the engine and coaches. The driver, fireman, guard and porter at Woodstock were all found guilty, severely reprimanded and suspended without pay until 17 November 1897.

The first passenger services offered five trains each way daily and an early morning goods train on weekdays only, all trains being allowed 10 minutes for the 3¾ miles. By 1910 the number of trains had increased to eight each way taking 8 minutes. The frequency was nine in 1922, while by 1938 only three trains ran through to Oxford. Service timetable appendices for 1945 revealed that signal lamps on the branch were not to be lit from 1 June till 31 July.

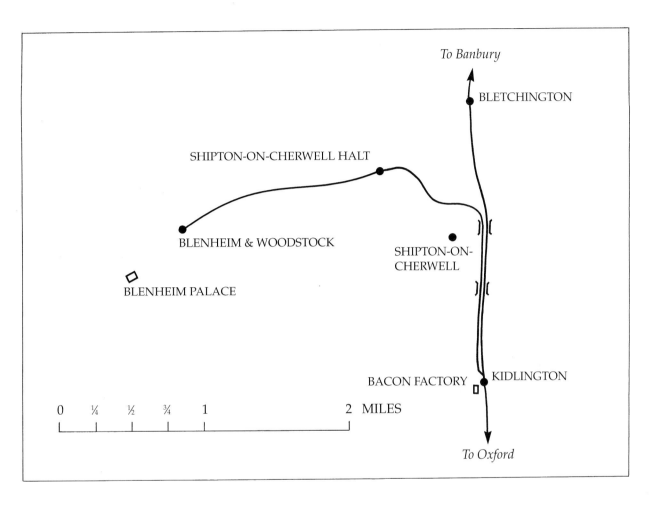

A 517 class 0–4–2T, No. 1473 *Fair Rosamund*, at Oxford with a through train to Blenheim & Woodstock. The engine is hauling an autotrailer.

c. 1920 Author's collection

A 4–4–0, No. 3806 *County Kildare*, at Kidlington on a Down stopping train from Oxford to Banbury. *Fair Rosamund* is on the branch auto train.

1930 Lens of Sutton

Trellis work around the garden on the Up platform, Kidlington.

c. 1910 Author's collection

Fair Rosamund at Blenheim & Woodstock with the Royal train, which carried the Prince of Wales.

23.11.1896 Author's collection

Blenheim & Woodstock station. Notice the engine shed and signal-box beyond. In the foreground and on the right-hand platform are well-kept flower beds.

c. 1910 Lens of Sutton

Fair Rosamund and autotrailer No. 119, ex-steam railmotor No. 23.

10.5.30 H.C. Casserley

A 517 class 0–4–2T, No. 1159, and autotrailer No. 110, ex-steam railmotor No. 12. No. 1159 was withdrawn in August 1947.

c. 1947 J.H. Russell

A 48XX class 0–4–2T, No. 4843, at Blenheim & Woodstock. The autotrailer gleams.

24.6.35 Lens of Sutton

A 54XX class 0–6–0PT, No. 5413, at Blenheim & Woodstock.

c. 1953 P.Q. Treloar collection

The exterior of Blenheim & Woodstock station.

c. 1910 Author's collection

Oxford to Launton

The Oxford & Bletchley Junction Railway was authorized in 1846 to construct a line to Oxford from the LNWR's London to Birmingham line at Bletchley. On 22 July 1847 the company was amalgamated with the Buckingham & Brackley Junction Railway, also authorized in 1846, to form the Buckinghamshire Railway. Not all were in favour of the line. There was a serious disturbance at Bicester when a farmer, Mr Dodwell, confronted the railway's surveyors, and another clash occurred at Islip between surveyors and villagers.

The Buckinghamshire Railway opened from Verney Junction to Islip on 1 October 1850; Islip to Banbury Road 3½ miles from Oxford on 2 December 1850; and to Oxford on 20 May 1851. The latter opening was celebrated by a luncheon for four hundred, attended by the directors and other notabilities. The first train to leave Oxford was a special, which carried a large number of passengers at reduced fares to visit the Great Exhibition in Hyde Park. It ran the 78 miles to Euston in 1 hour 50 minutes. From 1 July 1851 the Buckinghamshire Railway was leased to the LNWR for a period of 999 years.

In 1853 the LNWR obtained an Act for building the Buckinghamshire Junction Railway, a 1¾ mile long line for linking the Buckinghamshire Railway with the OWWR at Yarnton. This line, usually called the Yarnton Loop, had standard gauge double track and opened on 1 April 1854. In September 1853, to make full use of this line, John Parson, the OWWR's dubious solicitor who had become the railway's deputy chairman, made an agreement with Capt. Mark Huish, the LNWR's manager, to divert all OWWR London traffic from the GWR to the LNWR. Handborough was adapted to become the OWWR junction station by opening extra sidings and a refreshment room. Four standard gauge trains ran each way with Worcester to Euston through coaches. LNWR engines worked through to Handborough, where they collected through coaches and took them to Bletchley, where they were attached to Up trains for the rest of their journey. Meanwhile, the OWWR drew the rest to the GWR station at Oxford. A curve, the South-West Junction at the Bletchley end of the Yarnton Loop, gave access to the LNWR at Oxford without reversal. All OWWR freight trains for Oxford had to use the LNWR's Oxford, Rewley Road, station, as the GWR's St Aldate's goods station was only laid with broad gauge rails. OWWR passenger trains had a choice of either the LNWR or the GWR passenger station. It is believed that OWWR passenger trains only availed themselves of this facility from October until December 1857.

In return for offering traffic to the LNWR, the LNWR considered the distance between Euston and Yarnton Junction (there was no station at Yarnton at this period, one not being provided until the Witney branch opened in 1861) as 65 instead of the 76 true miles; accommodated OWWR trains at Rewley Road; and undertook to develop passenger traffic by 'express or other quick trains'. The fastest train from Euston to

Worcester took 4 hours for the 129¼ real miles. This through service ceased at the end of September 1861 when the Oxford to Worcester line was leased to the GWR. After a few years the South-West Junction became redundant and so was closed in 1863.

The secretary of the Buckinghamshire Railway was Edward Watkin, a far-sighted man. In 1853 he was appointed general manager of the Manchester, Sheffield & Lincolnshire Railway (MS&LR), becoming chairman in 1864. Not long after he was also made chairman of the South Eastern Railway and the Metropolitan Railway. With the vision of running through trains from Manchester to the continent, he formed the Channel Tunnel Company in 1872 and excavation work started in 1881. The MS&LR built an extension to London and became the Great Central Railway. However, by the time the extension was completed in 1899, the relationship with the southern companies had changed and his vast scheme remained incomplete. Watkin was knighted in 1868 and created a baronet in 1880.

For the introduction of the Oxford to Bicester steam railmotor service in October 1905, halts were opened at Port Meadow, Wolvercote, Oxford Road, Oddington, Charlton and Wendlebury. The branch proved to be a vital link in both wars. In August 1914, twelve trains conveyed a Yeomanry brigade en route from Cromer to Churn, and throughout the First World War hundreds of troop trains passed over the branch, including some carrying Russians.

The opening on 8 November 1940 of a direct south-facing double-track junction, just north of the station at Oxford, facilitated the development of through traffic, as hitherto the route had been via an exchange siding with a rising gradient towards the GWR of about 1 in 30 for a few yards. This loop had a maximum capacity of only twenty-two wagons. Principally it had been used for the interchange of goods vehicles and for LMS Express Mail vans labelled 'Glasgow (Central) and Southampton'. In 1942, to assist working the new junction, sidings were laid at Port Meadow where trains awaiting a path to GWR metals could remain without blocking LMS passenger traffic. The link was most useful in diverting north–south traffic away from London, and proved especially valuable in the period leading up to D-Day. Traffic for the South Eastern Section of the Southern Railway from the Great Northern and Great Eastern sections of the LNER, and also from the MR and LNWR sections of the LMS, were routed via Bletchley and Oxford to the GWR, and from there on to the South Eastern at Reading.

Bicester Central Ordnance Depot sidings, which were opened in 1941, brought further traffic. In the mid-1950s, freight was diverted over the branch to keep as much as possible away from London. The line was dieselized in the early 1960s, but this failed to stop the decline in passenger traffic and the last train ran on 30 December 1967. Meanwhile, the last train had run over the Yarnton Loop on 29 October 1965, and this line was taken out of use on 26 October 1966. Double track was no longer necessary for the reduced traffic, and the Oxford to Bicester branch was singled in October 1973. Oxford North Junction, ½ mile north of Rewley Road, closed on 29 October 1973. Access to Rewley Road was maintained through a siding and a new Oxford North Junction running into the Up loop, just over ½ mile to the north of the old junction. The line from Bicester to Claydon was singled on 24 June 1985.

On 11 May 1985 a special shoppers' train was run from Bicester to Oxford, hauled by No. 47618 *Fair Rosamund*. The experiment proving a success, the line reopened permanently to passengers on 11 May 1987, with a new intermediate station, costing £60,000, being opened at Islip on 15 May 1989.

Launton had a brick station building on its Down platform, with a timber-built ladies' waiting room. The platform was rather low, so portable wooden steps were provided for the less agile. The Up platform was of timber. No signal-box was provided, the levers being on an open raised frame on the platform. The station closed to goods trains on 30 November 1959. West of the station a trailing siding from the Up line led to Air Ministry property. This was in use from 1 October 1926 until 28 August 1957.

Immediately before the branch passed below the Aynho Junction to Princes Risborough line were the Southern Gas Board new sidings, opened on 19 February 1968 to serve a modern steam naphtha reforming plant. Rail traffic ceased in August 1971 and the sidings were taken out of use on 23 March 1984. They were worked by a John Fowler 0–4–0 diesel-mechanical locomotive.

Bicester was one of the two most important stations on the branch (Verney Junction was the other), and all trains were booked to stop there. 'London Road' was added to its title in March 1954. It had a twin-pavilion style building constructed of stone on the Up platform and a waiting shelter on the Down. The goods sidings were taken out of use on 9 June 1986 and the signal-box by the level-crossing was closed on the same day. All that is left of the old passenger station building is the limestone wall facing the platform. Today a bus stop type waiting shelter is set unusually at right angles to the track. The station is now the terminus of the hourly shuttle service from Oxford, a straight length of track allowing passengers to see a train about 3 miles distant.

South of the station is the line to the Bicester Military Railway. Wendlebury was a railmotor halt, though in accordance with LNWR practice the word halt did not appear in the title. Like all the other halts on the branch, it had a very low-level timber-built platform of about one coach length. Charlton and Oddington were similar halts.

Islip station was constructed entirely of timber. No signal-box was provided, the levers being on an open, raised platform. In April 1965 the passenger platforms were shortened to 130 ft. Goods sidings led off the Down line at both ends of the passenger platform. The station closed to goods on 7 September 1964, when it became a coal depot only until 1 January 1968. An aviation fuel siding trailing from the Up line, which was opened in 1941, still remains in situ. A capstan was used for shunting the petrol wagons. With the reopening of the line to passengers, a new platform was built with a bus stop type waiting shelter. A free car park is provided.

South of the station the line crosses Millstream No. 1 Viaduct, which is 59 yd in length, followed by Millstream No. 2 Viaduct, which is 85 yd long and crosses the River Cherwell.

The halt at Oxford Road had staggered platforms: the Down platform on the Oxford side of the level-crossing and the Up platform on the Bletchley side. The crossing was replaced by a bridge in 1935. Beyond the halt the Yarnton Loop left the main line and ran parallel with the Oxford line for 220 yd. Until February 1876 the junction had been where the loop curved from the main line, but that month the economy was made of controlling both junction and level-crossing from one signal-box. A writer in 1910 said that 'an immense coal traffic from South Wales' used the Yarnton Loop en route to the Midlands, 7,500 coal wagons utilizing it in March of that year. Although the loop was owned and maintained by the LMS to Yarnton Junction, by 1931 practice was for traffic to and from the GWR to be exchanged midway at Woodstock Road Crossing, both companies pushing wagons to this point. At Yarnton, eight exchange sidings, parallel with the Fairford branch, were brought into use on 20 August 1940 and a turntable was installed to enable locomotives to take a return load chimney-first. Brick trains used the route until the 1960s. Eastern Region engines seen at Yarnton include B1 class 4–6–0s, K3 2–6–0s and J39 0–6–0s.

Adjacent to Oxford Road Junction was a Ministry of Works grain silo, with rail access

Entry in *Bradshaw's Railway Manual, Shareholders' Guide & Directory*, 1865.

from 1943 until 1967. It was worked by an F.C. Hibberd and Co. Ltd four-wheel petrol-mechanical locomotive. From 1972 the site was used for an Amey Roadstone terminal, known in its last working days as Oxford, Banbury Road.

Until 1863 the South-West Junction curve trailed in, and beyond was Wolvercote Tunnel, which was 145 yd in length, before Wolvercote Halt was reached. On its adjacent line the GWR dropped the final 'e' from the name-board of its stopping place. Beyond, the line runs parallel with the GWR for the remaining 1¾ miles to Oxford. This stretch of line was used for unofficial racing. In 1931 the 11.35 a.m. LMS and the GWR 11.37 a.m. often provided a close race, while the 12.45 p.m. Paddington to Kingham, which passed Oxford at 1.54 a.m., competed with the 1.55 p.m. from Rewley Road.

Beyond Port Meadow Loops, which were in use from 1942 until 1960, was the halt at Summertown, renamed Port Meadow on 1 July 1907. It was built adjacent to Port Meadow, which separated the railway from the River Thames. On one occasion the halt proved particularly useful for a group of undergraduates who were returning on the Thursdays- and Saturdays-only railmotor. This left Bicester at 11.40 p.m. and, after travelling non-stop, was scheduled to arrive at Rewley Road at 12.05 a.m., well after the 10.00 p.m. deadline by which time they should have been back in college. The proctors waited at Rewley Road for their return, but a friendly porter had sent a message up the line to an equally complaisant signalman, with the result that the train stopped at Port

Meadow for the undergraduates to detrain, slip into college and avoid a gating. The surprised proctors met an empty train.

Rewley Road station on the site of Rewley Abbey, a Cistercian monastery, was built from prefabricated iron sections in 1851–2 by Fox, Henderson & Partners, contractors for the 1851 Crystal Palace, using the principles evolved by Paxton. Originally the train shed roof was glazed longitudinally and rested on diagonally braced girders and side columns, the latter clad with boarding. In 1888 the glazing was changed to a lateral, north light pattern. The entrance building was of timber, as was the single 450 ft long, double-sided platform. Incoming trains used the right-hand road, but either platform was used for departures. As there was no room in the train shed for a crossover, the station pilot was required to draw coaches out in order to release the engine. In the station's early years, the platform roads and sidings were connected by rolling-stock turntables. When the low, six-wheeled coaches were withdrawn, the platform was raised to standard height and paved. The circular booking office, also used as the stationmaster's office, is said to have come from the Great Exhibition of 1851.

Following its closure to passengers on 1 October 1951, when trains were diverted to the Up or Down bays at Oxford General (the former GWR station), Rewley Road station was used as a railway hostel and the train shed was subsequently removed. In the late 1960s its use as a hostel ceased and the building was taken over by a tyre firm, which still uses it. The only surviving example of its type, the remaining main building and canopy are Grade II listed. The stationmaster's house used to be near the entrance, and a long row of coal merchants' offices was built by the LNWR.

After the diversion of passenger traffic, the former LNWR goods yard remained in use for the reception of most of the city's coal. Other traffic included cattle cake and products for the Shell-Mex depot. The goods shed sidings were taken out of use in August 1966. On 22 November 1969 the layout was rationalized, and the yard was closed entirely on 5 April 1984.

Situated at the station throat was an 85 ton steel swing-bridge, which spanned the 40 ft wide Rewley Abbey Stream, alternatively known as the Sheepwash Channel. The 73 ft bridge swung on a central turntable carried on rollers. It was hand-worked and in 1907 was opened about six times daily. Well-balanced at first, two men could easily open and close it in 4 or 5 minutes by turning a crank on a pedestal either side of the bridge centre. Latterly, six to eight men were required.

Before the bridge could be opened, the signalman in the adjacent Rewley Road signal-box first blocked back to Oxford Road signal-box to prevent any train from leaving Oxford or Oxford Road. After all signals had been placed at danger, he pulled a lever that unlocked two bolts and released the bridge, simultaneously locking all points and signals at the station. Steel blocks, placed in position and released by hand gearing, were provided at each end of the bridge to ensure rigidity when trains passed over. A higher level, fixed-position, small bridge carried point rodding and signal wires alongside the swing-bridge.

With the opening of the branch in 1851, there was a three-road engine shed built of corrugated iron that stabled up to nine locomotives. In 1855, five engines were in steam daily with two held in reserve. Adjacent was a 16,000 gallon tank to which water was raised by steam pump from the River Thames, which ran alongside the shed. A gale on 14 October 1877 removed much of the shed roof. It was repaired, but then on 15 June 1879 the workshop and part of the shed were damaged by fire. Further repairs were undertaken, but by 1883 the structure was demolished and replaced with a standard Webb northlight pattern in brick, which cost £1,817. With two roads of 150 ft in length, the shed only stabled six engines. The 42 ft diameter turntable was replaced by one of 50 ft in 1928. No coaling

Launton, view Down. Notice the steps to assist disabled passengers to and from the low-level platform. The oil lamp and its casing is worth a second glance.

c. 1950 Lens of Sutton

stage was provided until March 1950, and the shed closed on 3 December that same year. The locomotives together with between twenty and thirty men were transferred to the former GWR shed on the opposite side of the line. The LNWR shed had been a sub-shed of Bletchley.

Early in the twentieth century, 'Lady of the Lake' class 2–2–2s, 5 ft 6 in 2–4–2Ts and Webb 0–6–2Ts worked the line, the latter lasting till the 1940s. At one time, two of the 2–2–2s at Oxford in use on passenger and milk trains were *Daphne* and *Prince Alfred*. 'Precursor' class 4–4–0s appeared before 1914. By 1930 a variety of engines was seen: 2–4–0 'Precedents', 4–4–0 'Precursors', 'George the Fifths', 4–6–0 'Experiments' and the 8800 mixed traffic class. No. 5031 *Hardwicke* of the 1895 Race to Aberdeen fame was frequently seen. A 6700 class 2–4–2T usually worked the tightest train schedule of the day – the 10.45 a.m. Down – because with a light load this type was considered by drivers to be the fastest engine. The LMS imposed a low limit for these engines of two non-corridor coaches per train, together with any empties or horsebox traffic to a maximum of 220 tons. The longest surviving member of its class, 4–6–0 No. 25845 *Prince of Wales* worked regularly over the branch until it was withdrawn in November 1947.

Goods trains were worked by Super D 0–8–0s, 'Cauliflower' 0–6–0s and 0–6–2T 'Coal Tanks', while LYR and LMS Class 4F 0–6–0s made an occasional appearance. At Rewley Road, 0–6–0STs were used for shunting.

In 1934, Deeley Compound No. 1102 appeared on a Colne to Oxford excursion. Johnson class 3P 4–4–0s appeared, as did Class 3F 0–6–0Ts, while during the Second World War US-built Class S160 2–8–0s worked over the branch. Stream-lined Pacific

110

No. 6220 *Coronation* visited Oxford for publicity purposes in 1937. In 1941, Dean 0–6–0 No. 2529, displaying that number on the cabside and WD No. 156 on the tender, with the name 'Flying Fortress' inscribed above the smoke box door, appeared at Rewley Road shed almost daily, having come from Bicester Military Railway.

Stanier 2–6–4T No. 42667 worked the last passenger train from Rewley Road, the 4.45 p.m. to Bletchley, on 1 October 1951. In the 1950s and '60s, engines often seen included ex-LNWR G1 and G2 class 0–8–0s, ex-LMS Class 5 2–6–0s and 4–6–0s, and Class 8F 2–8–0s. BR Standard Class 4 4–6–0s and 9F 2–10–0s, ex-Great Eastern D16 4–4–0s, LNER B1 class 4–6–0s, K3 2–6–0s and GER B12 class 4–6–0s worked Oxford to Cambridge trains in the 1950s, while occasionally 0–6–0s of the J19 and J37 classes made an appearance. Steam ceased in 1965 with the closure of the Oxford and Bletchley depots.

The LNWR began a steam railmotor service between Oxford and Bicester in October 1905, opening six special halts. The company only possessed six railmotors – few for such a large concern. The engine units were manufactured at Crewe and the coachwork at Wolverton using many standard coach parts. Owing to wartime economies, the railmotors were withdrawn and the halts closed on 1 January 1917, but they were restored on 5 May 1919, only for the service to be finally withdrawn and the halts closed on 25 October 1926 as a result of the General Strike.

These railmotors had three unusual features:
• The driver's compartment had double doors at the front end, through which the engine could be drawn for repair. The upper halves of these doors were louvred to improve ventilation, always a bugbear with railcars of other designs.
• The railmotor had inside cylinders in contrast with all other British railways, which used outside cylinders on their motors.
• The folding steps that gave access at low-level halts curiously folded sideways, instead of vertically like those on other company's railmotors. As was general practice, for safety the steps were interlocked with the vacuum brake, because if they were left down they fouled the loading gauge.

The passenger saloon was divided into two compartments: smoking and non-smoking. Each compartment seated twenty-four third-class passengers and had three windows. They were modern vehicles equipped with electric lighting. Railcars No. 1 to No. 3 had three windows on each side of the engine compartment, but these were altered to louvres to improve the ventilation. No. 4 to No. 6 were so built from the start.

No. 2 and No. 3, which were built in 1905, were sent new to work from Oxford to Bicester. No. 3 was later transferred to the Bangor to Bethesda branch, and eventually all of the railcars were moved to North Wales. No. 3 lasted into BR days, being withdrawn in February 1948. It was only outlasted by a L&YR railmotor.

The branch saw two interesting internal combustion engine vehicles in the 1930s. Early in 1932 a Micheline unit was tested between Bletchley and Oxford. The first rail vehicle in Britain to use pneumatic tyres, it was carried on a six-wheel bogie (six wheels were required due to the comparatively narrow tread of a standard rail) at the front and a four-wheel bogie at the rear. The centre pair of front bogie wheels were drivers, chain-connected to the front pair. The pneumatic tyres had a metal flange on each inside rim. A gauge on each wheel monitored the air pressure. If it fell in excess of 14 lb per sq. inch below the normal 85 psi, an audible warning system sounded. In the event of a burst tyre, a wooden hoop within took the load. A tyre lasted for about 20,000 miles. The spare wheel and tyre carried on board could be fitted in about 5 minutes.

A 27 hp Panhard & Levassor engine drove through a clutch and gear box. Separate reverse gears permitted four speeds in either direction, but as the railcar could only be driven from the front, reverse was only used when shunting. Lockheed hydraulic brakes worked shoes on drums. Aircraft-type water-cooled radiators were attached each side of the driving cab roof. A saloon of 21 ft by 8 ft could accommodate twenty-four passengers. It could be heated by passing air over the exhaust. The overall length of the railcar was 44 ft 9 in and its width was 8 ft 7 in. Between Bletchley and Oxford from a standstill and with a full load, the car reached 60 m.p.h. in 2 minutes. It ran almost silently and had a petrol consumption of 12 m.p.g.

Early in 1938, Derby Carriage & Wagon Works completed a three-car, articulated diesel train – Nos 8000, 8001 and 8002 – which ran trials between Oxford and Cambridge. The bodies consisted of timber frames with outer panels of steel welded together. To reduce air resistance, the gaps between the coaches were covered by rubber sheeting. The set was painted in a livery of aluminium and Post Office red, and it was driven by six Leyland 125 b.h.p. diesel engines through Lysholm-Smith torque converters. Two engines were below each car driving the inner axles of adjacent bogies, thus only the two outer axles were unpowered. The axles turned on SKF roller bearings. Brakes were on the Westinghouse compressed air system, the shoes having Ferodo linings. The train's maximum speed was 75 m.p.h. and the total weight of the three-car set was 73 tons.

Both end coaches had two third-class compartments, which seated twenty-six smoking and twenty-eight non-smoking passengers. The centre coach had three compartments which seated thirty-two third-class smoking, sixteen first-class smoking and eight first-class non-smoking passengers. All seats were transverse and, except for those against partitions, had tramway-style reversible backs to allow passengers to face the direction of travel. On chromium-plated steel tubular frames were cushions upholstered with uncut moquette with a Dunlopillo filling. Heating was from a Clarkson boiler, the heat being supplied from the exhaust of the engines of the end cars. Air-operated sliding doors were controlled by the guard. Buffers and drawgear were for emergency use only – the unit was not intended to work in multiple. Detachable oval buffer faces were carried, and could be secured by pins to the existing tube-shape buffers to enable the unit to be coupled to an ordinary locomotive or rolling-stock. These buffer heads were removed in normal use to reduce wind resistance.

Trials on the branch led to several modifications: the streamlined panels between the bogies were removed; and a wire grille was fitted in front of the driver's window to prevent shattering by, say, a lump of coal falling from a passing tender. Withdrawn at the outbreak of the Second World War, the train was stored until 1949, when it was converted to a two-car maintenance train for the Manchester South Junction & Altrincham electric line.

In 1887, seven trains ran each way and one on Sundays, taking 24 minutes for the 12 miles to Bicester. An express service of three through trains to Cambridge was inaugurated on 1 March 1905, the fastest taking 2 hours 25 minutes – a vast improvement on the change and wait at Bletchley, when a journey could take 5–6 hours, most passengers finding it better to travel via London. By 1910 the frequency of branch trains had increased to fourteen Down and fifteen Up (including six railmotors in each direction), and one each way on Sundays. Railmotors took 35 minutes as they called at the six halts in addition to Islip station. The 1922 timetable showed little alteration except that three trains ran on Sundays. By 1938 the weekly service had fallen to eleven Down and nine Up, but that on Sundays had increased to four. The normal journey time was reduced to 20 minutes. In 1967, ten trains ran daily between Oxford and Cambridge, the fastest taking just over 2 hours for the 77 miles. Each week, 3,000 passengers used the branch from Oxford and 2,000 from Bicester.

In about 1900 the two goods drivers at Oxford worked week and week about the day and night pick-up goods service to Bletchley and back, their duty demanding a 12 hour turn and often more. In 1930, goods trains ran from Oxford Road Junction to Bletchley at approximately three-hourly intervals day and night, most carrying coal brought by the GWR from South Wales to Yarnton Junction. All were worked over the branch by Bletchley men. In 1959, as well as two local goods trains there were through goods trains: Wellingborough to Yarnton, Ipswich to Cardiff, Cambridge to Cardiff, Irthlingborough to Yarnton and Corby sidings to Hinksey.

Today, in addition to the passenger service of twelve each way on weekdays and four on Sundays, the Avon County Council rubbish train en route from Bath and Bristol to Calvert runs over the branch, and in April 1995 the rubbish train from Northolt was diverted due to a bridge defect in the Aylesbury area. RfD runs a Monday to Friday service to the military depot at Bicester, and from late September till mid-April Mainline operates a block coal train from the Midlands to Bicester Camp.

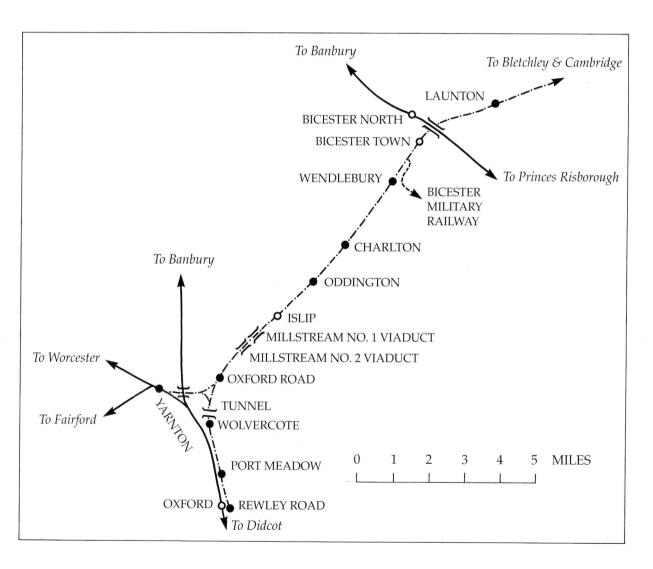

Two-car Derby Lightweight DMU, 1 mile west of Launton, working the 10.43 Cambridge to Oxford train.

24.6.66 Michael Mensing

Bicester, view Up. Notice the porters' walkway between the two platforms.

c. 1905 Author's collection

The LMS Bicester sign, with 'London Road' added subsequently; view Up.

c. 1950 Lens of Sutton

A Derby Lightweight DMU for Oxford enters Bicester London Road station.

30.12.67 E. Wilmshurst

The plaque on Bicester Town station reads: 'Thames. Councillor Bryn Duggan, Chairman, Oxfordshire County Council unveiled this plaque on 13 May 1989 marking the improvements to the train service between Bicester and Oxford, made possible by funding from Oxfordshire County Council, Cherwell District Council, Oxford City Council and Network SouthEast.'

21.4.95 Author

Islip, view Down. Notice the two signal arms on one post, the timber platforms and the rows of fifteen milk churns. The signal levers stand in the open on the left of the main timber building.

c. 1905 Lens of Sutton

Islip, view towards Oxford.

21.4.95 Author

Class 165/1 Network Turbo No. 165121 at Islip with the 13.51 Bicester Town to Oxford train.
21.4.95 Author

Rail level halt at Wendlebury during a test run of LNWR railmotor No. 2 before the line was opened in October 1905. The notice on the left reads: 'Beware of Trains. Look both Up and Down the line before you cross.' The driver is leaning from his labelled door, his fireman to the right.
October 1905 Lens of Sutton

Ex-LNER B12 class 4–6–0 No. 61546 leaves Oxford with a train to Cambridge. It has left the GWR line (right) and is on LMS metals.

March 1959 P.Q. Treloar

LMS Class 2MT 2–6–0 No. 46465 leaving Oxford with a Cambridge train.

November 1959 P.Q. Treloar

A 61XX class 2–6–2T, No. 6138, at Port Meadow, having worked from Bicester with a military freight.

c. 1959 P.Q. Treloar

Ex-LMS Class 8F 2–8–0 nears Oxford with a Bletchley line freight.

c. 1959 P.Q. Treloar

A 2–4–0 Precedent class, No. 1668 *Dagmar*, with a Down train at Port Meadow Halt. Built in March 1868, this engine was withdrawn in 1932 as LMS No. 5023. The GWR is on the left.

c. 1914 P.Q. Treloar collection

The frontage of Rewley Road station.

c. 1910 Author's collection

The frontage of Rewley Road station, now a tyre depot.

21.4.95 Author

The interior of Rewley Road station, view outwards towards Bicester.

1914 Author's collection

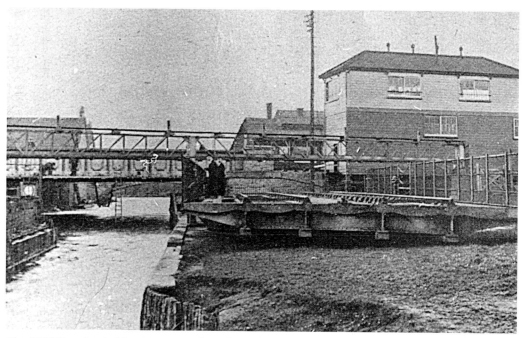

The LNWR swing-bridge is open and on the right bank. The fixed bridge at a higher level carries signal wires and point rodding. Behind is the GWR Oxford Station North signal-box.

c 1905 Author's collection

The swing-bridge, view Up. Although the bridge still has two tracks, only one is in use. The notice reads: 'Notice to Staff. Before allowing a train to cross the swingbridge the bearing blocks at each end must be in the fully raised position. Also ensure that the bearing blocks are lowered before attempting to open or close the swingbridge.' A pedestal in the centre of the bridge carries two pinions to which handles are fixed for swinging the bridge. The higher level bridge is on the left.

27.6.81 Author

Caledonian Railway 4–2–2 No. 123 and GWR 4–4–0 No. 3440 *City of Truro* in Rewley Road yard, Oxford.

29.4.60 P.Q. Treloar

Articulated diesel set Car Nos 80000/1/2 at Rewley Road, Oxford. The white 'V' is the rear of a gradient post. The continuous panelling over the body gaps presents the appearance of a single unit.

c. 1938 Lens of Sutton

Ex-LNER D15 class 4–4–0 No. 62576 at Oxford with an educational special from Cambridge.
7.8.57 Revd Alan Newman

A two-car DMU working the 2.26 p.m. to Cambridge leaves Oxford during the second week of diesel operation.
11.11.59 P.Q. Treloar

Bicester Military Railway

The site south of Bicester was chosen for this large depot as it was convenient for rail access and the land was of low agricultural value. Construction started in the summer of 1941, the plan being to lay the track and then bring in materials for erecting the storehouses. Just inside the gate leading from the LMS to War Department property were the exchange sidings. The first access to these was by ground frame, which was opened on 13 July 1941, at the Oxford end of the layout, and on 9 November the same year, Bicester No. 2 signal-box was opened at the other end. By the spring of 1942, work was sufficiently complete for main line empty coaching stock to be taken into the depot for troops to entrain.

The basic track plan of the depot resembles a pair of spectacles: a circle round Graven Hill serves D and E sites; a circle round Arncott serves the MT (Motor Transport) sidings and B and C sites; and these two circles are linked by a main line of 2 miles in length. From Arncott a branch extends to Piddington, ending only ¼ mile from the GWR's Banbury to Princes Risborough line with which at one time it was intended to connect.

Soldiers were transported to work sites by train in open wagons, civilians enjoying rather superior accommodation in old French Ferry vans. In 1943, three-coach sets were provided for internal traffic – both workmen's and recreational – to concerts, film shows and dances. At its height the service carried more than 32,000 passengers a week. Workmen's trains ran in the morning, at midday and in the evening, taking precedence over freight trains as the loss of man-hours caused by even a 5 minute delay would have been considerable. At one time 24,000 troops were at Bicester Depot.

Traffic was hectic in preparation for D-Day, including tanks, guns, small arms and motor transport. The MT sidings were built to relieve congestion at Arncott Yard and held wagons when there was a storehouse blockage. At one time 238 wagons were held for B4 shed alone. The four sidings were laid within a week.

At first the LMS provided coaches and motive power for a regular evening service from Banbury Camp to Oxford, but owing to wartime stock and manpower shortages, the LMS found it impossible to continue this service and said that if the Army desired the train it must provide staff, rolling-stock and a locomotive. The Sappers took up this challenge. Booked time from Bicester LMS station to Oxford, Rewley Road, was 20 minutes for the 12 miles, but 16 minutes was the norm for a Sapper driver of a WD locomotive and the record was said to be held by an ex-SR 0–4–2 No. 625 hauling eight coaches. To stop this train speeding, the LMS district inspector eventually had to instruct his signalmen to keep all distant signals at danger when this train was due! Following the end of hostilities, the National Union of Railwaymen insisted that LMS crews took this train to Oxford. It continued running until the early 1960s.

A special weekend troop train from Bicester Depot ran to Euston each Friday with up to twelve coaches divided into two parts when working over the camp lines. On Sunday evening the Euston announcer would say over the public address system: 'The train standing at the platform is the 10 o'clock – the first portion for Arncott and Piddington; the rear coaches for Graven Hill and Ambrosden'. There was also a weekend through train to and from the north. Sunday night's passenger traffic at Piddington was very busy with one train to Oxford, two to Bicester, one from Oxford, two from Bicester, one from Euston and one from the North. Troops travelled free to Bicester and could go to Oxford for 6d return.

The single main line between Graven Hill Depot and Arncott Depot has a signal-box at each end. Today the electric single line tokens are stamped with 'Glen Douglas–Garelochhead', revealing their origin. The rest of the line is controlled by regulator and telephone, and when a driver reaches the end of a section he phones to ask for permission to enter the next section.

The 45 miles of track were originally laid with 75 lb/yd rail on spent ash ballast 9 inches deep, and as it is mainly above clay, this pumps through in places. Much of the original rail and ballast is still in use 53 years later, though in 1990 the main line was relaid with 113 lb/yd rail on stone ballast. The track distance has now been reduced to 43 miles. Although most sleepers are concrete, some are steel and intended for laying on desert sand. Because of their rounded shape, ballast cannot be packed under sleepers of this pattern and this leads to unevenness in the road bed as they are unsupported where the most weight is experienced. In places where the metal rail retaining keys have gone, timber sleepers replace every fifth sleeper to keep the track to gauge.

Currently the depot is served by one Class 37 hauled RfD train daily. In addition to stores taken in and out, a total of 500–600 HEA bottom-discharging wagons, each containing 27 tons of coal, arrive during the heating season for the three boiler-houses, which supply heat to the vast storage sheds. Several container trains have worked from Bicester and then through the Channel Tunnel to Germany.

Today, 270 rolling-stock vehicles are provided for internal use, some dating back 50 years. Painted in Brunswick green livery, some of the vans have yellow ends to aid visibility. As not all wagons are continuously braked, brake vans are coupled to the rear. Three brake vans are ex-BR Standard vehicles and one is an SR type built for the War Department. At Bicester there is a London & South Western Railway (LSWR) coach that was built in 1907. It was used as an ambulance coach during the Second World War and converted at Bicester to have an observation end. It is painted in GWR colours and carried Queen Elizabeth II when she visited the depot on 16 May 1978.

The first locomotives at Bicester were two ex-GWR 'Dean Goods' 0–6–0s No. 2485 and No. 2529, and the stud was increased by the arrival of LSWR Adams A12 class 0–4–2 No. 625. In mid-1943 the first Austerity class 0–6–0STs arrived and these frequently hauled trains of a hundred wagons in length from Graven Hill to Arncott, or vice versa. Barclay 0–8–0DHs with twin Cummins diesel engines replaced the Austerities in 1965. In turn these gave way to four-wheel diesel-hydraulic Vanguards in 1982, eventually their Rolls-Royce engines being replaced by those of Cummins' manufacture. Today, five Steelman Royale four-wheel diesel-hydraulics operate the line. Normally three are in use; a fourth is kept for special runs, while the fifth has non-technical maintenance – greasing and cleaning – undertaken by its driver. Each driver has his own engine and takes great pride in keeping it looking like new. Arncott workshops, once the central workshops for all of the War Department locomotives, closed in 1982. Until about 1960 when a locomotive shed was built at Graven Hill, it also housed the Bicester engines.

Current locomotive stock at Bicester, all Steelman Royale four-wheel diesel-hydraulic 335 hp locomotives built by Thomas Hill:

No.	Class	Works No.	Year built
270	Greensleeves	V318	1987
271	Storeman	V324	1987
272	Royal Pioneer	V320	1987
275	Sapper	V323	1987
276	Conductor	V319	1987

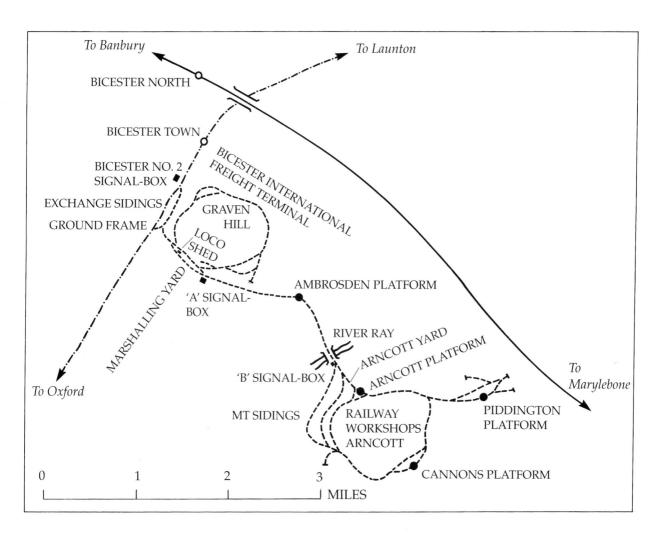

A Locomotive Club of Great Britain special, hauled by Austerity class 0–6–0ST No. 197 *Sapper*. Behind the engine is a brake van built for the War Department by the SR. The last coach is an LSWR vehicle, built in 1907.

23.9.72 E. Wilmshurst

The Royal train, hauled by a Barclay 0–8–0DH, passing B2 building, Arncott.

16.8.78 Author's collection

A 1907 LSWR coach converted to an observation saloon by the War Department sometime after 1958. This photograph was taken inside the engine shed.

31.5.95 Author

Barclay 0–8–0DH No. 625 *Craftsman* outside the locomotive shed.

23.9.72 E. Wilmshurst

A steam crane. Notice the chimney folded down to prevent it from fouling the loading gauge.

c. 1965 Author's collection

A view of Graven Hill 'A' signal-box from the cab of No. 276 *Conductor*. The signalman waits to collect the single-line tablet.

31.5.95 Author

Tyer's No. 7 single-line tablet instrument in Graven Hill 'A' signal-box. The tablets are stamped 'Glen Douglas–Garelochhead'.

31.5.95 Author

Sorting Sidings platform built from concrete sleepers. Beyond, No. 275 *Sapper* is shunting pallet vans.

31.5.95 Author

Oxford to Kelmscott & Langford

The first proposals for the Oxford to Kelmscott & Langford line were made in 1836, when a rail link was planned between Cheltenham and London. This particular scheme was thwarted as were several subsequent projects, but eventually the Witney Railway, which had a keen supporter in Charles Early of blanket fame, proved feasible. A line was constructed from the OWWR at Yarnton to Witney. Apart from blankets, Witney was important for brewing, leather goods and its market.

The GWR opposed the Witney Railway bill and naturally resented the loop at Yarnton giving access to its competitor's line – the LNWR's Bletchley to Oxford branch. The GWR was afraid that the Witney line would eventually be extended to Cheltenham and siphon off its lucrative spa traffic. The protest was in vain, and the Witney Railway Act received Royal Assent on 1 August 1859.

Small railways like the Witney Railway did not usually purchase their own engines and rolling-stock but were worked by a larger company. On 17 May 1860 the OWWR agreed to work and maintain the line for a period of 10 years from the opening, in return for 50 per cent of gross receipts. On 1 July 1860 the OWWR became part of the West Midland Railway, which took over the agreement.

Messrs Pickering started constructing the line at Eynsham on 19 May 1860, and on 10 August the following year works were sufficiently advanced for the directors to travel the length of the line on an engine lent by the WMR. The railway was inspected by the Board of Trade on 5 November, and on the 14th it was opened to passenger traffic. Goods, except for coal, were not carried until 1 March 1862, because the goods sheds had not been built. Receipts for the first year allowed the modest dividend of 2 per cent to be paid on ordinary share capital. Subsequently, dividends fell to 1 per cent, and owners of the land the railway was built on pressed for payment.

Revenue was not up to expectations and a scapegoat had to be found. The GWR had absorbed the WMR on 1 August 1863 and it was alleged that the pattern of the train service aroused local ill will. The GWR's methods of accounting denied the Witney Company sums due to them. The Witney's solicitors examined minutely the GWR's accounts and discovered cause for complaint, but the GWR was unmoved. In 1866 the company's dividends ceased and the directors blamed the GWR, saying: 'Every year the line appears to carry increased traffic, but the returns show no corresponding improvement'.

In mid-1867 the Court of Chancery appointed the secretary of the company as receiver so that the claims of the landowners could be met. The railway remained in Chancery until 1875. In 1871 the working agreement was renewed on better terms, although the GWR protested that it showed a loss. After 1875, dividends were resumed, and they rose to as high as 4 per cent in the 1880s.

Meanwhile the East Gloucestershire Railway (EGR) Act had been passed on 7 August 1862. The EGR was to extend from Cheltenham to Witney, and the MR agreed to subscribe £100,000 towards the EGR and work the line when completed. The first sod was cut in a field near Cheltenham by Lady Russell, the wife of the chairman, on 31 March 1865. With a silver shovel she cut the sod, threw it quickly into a wheelbarrow and then beat a hasty retreat before a large, unruly crowd.

On 30 May Parliament refused the MR permission to subscribe to the EGR, which then placed the company in financial difficulties, and the contractors stopped work. An extension of time was granted on 15 July 1867 and a working agreement made with the GWR. In 1868 the EGR decided to postpone Cheltenham plans and confine itself to a Witney to Fairford line. It managed to find a contractor willing to take a large number of shares in lieu of payment and work started in May 1869. The completed line was opened on 15 January 1873. It was still hoped that the line would reach Cirencester or even Cheltenham, but the GWR was unwilling to give support and the EGR was not financially strong enough to carry out such a plan.

In 1906 the branch was the first single line on the GWR to be equipped for Automatic Train Control (ATC) working, which meant that a driver would receive an audible warning if he passed a signal at danger. Previous experiments had been on the double track Henley branch and the system required modification for use on a single line. So successful was it that every distant signal between Yarnton Junction and Fairford was abolished and replaced by an ATC ramp.

During the Second World War, Yarnton Junction became an important exchange point between the LMS and GWR. A nine-road yard opened in August 1940, and to facilitate operation a turntable was installed. Many RAF airfields opened in the area were served by the branch, and when RAF Brize Norton was extended, two aircraft taxiways crossed the line on the level. In the interests of safety, special signalling arrangements were made between the RAF control tower and Bampton signal-box. Extra-short telegraph posts were used to prevent them from being struck by low-flying aircraft.

Carterton station was opened on 2 October 1944 to deal with passengers to and from Brize Norton. In the period leading to D-Day the area had many supply dumps ready for the invasion, and good proportion of their contents arrived and departed by train.

The branch lost its passenger service on 18 June 1962, when the line beyond Witney closed completely. The remaining signal-boxes shut three weeks later and the branch was worked on the One Engine in Steam principle (only one engine is allowed on a single line to avoid a collision). Level-crossing gates were padlocked across the line and unlocked by a key attached to the wooden train staff. Marker boards beyond a crossing indicated the number of wagon lengths from the crossing. This meant that a driver would know where to stop clear of the crossing so that his guard could close the gates.

On 2 November 1970 the goods service was withdrawn from Witney and the 40,000 tons of freight carried annually went by road. Although the branch was officially closed, on 3 November a class 22 diesel collected the last mineral wagons from Witney.

Branch passenger trains started from a bay platform at the Down end of Oxford station. Yarnton Junction had two platforms. That on the Down side was designed as an island, but was fenced off from the goods loop. The timber and iron shelter was unique on the GWR. In 1929 the signal-box was converted from power to manual operation. Beyond the station, branch trains swung westwards away from the main line to Worcester.

Cassington Halt had a 100 ft long concrete platform cast at the GWR's concrete works in Taunton. On the platform was a timber waiting shelter, which was opened on 9 March

A 74XX class 0–6–0PT, No. 7436, heads a Down passenger train at Witney. Plenty of sacks await the Up train, the pile of mail bags beyond the signal-box nearly reaching the window sills.

c. 1960 Lens of Sutton

1936. In the late 1930s or 1947/8 it was moved to a new site a little to the west and on the opposite side of the line. This was necessary due to the rebuilding of the adjacent road bridge.

The sidings of Eynsham Sugar Beet & Crop Driers Ltd, which were opened in 1927, were 1½ miles beyond. They were worked by an 0–4–0ST built by Brush Electrical Engineering Ltd in 1906, works number 314. Formerly No. 6 of Powlesland & Mason, a firm which handled GWR traffic over the Swansea Harbour Trust's line, it became GWR No. 921 and was purchased by the Eynsham firm in September 1928. The sugar beet venture proved unsuccessful. In 1931 the factory closed and that December the engine was sold to Berry Wiggins & Co. Ltd of Kingsnorth in Kent. The engine ceased working there in 1964 and by June 1967 it had reached Leicester Museum. During the Second World War the site at Eynsham was the Royal Army Service Corps Depot and it had five looped sidings, while in 1950 it was used by the Colonial Development Corporation, but the property was sold and the sidings taken out of use in 1956.

Eynsham station was ½ mile beyond. The weatherboarded, hipped roof station building was constructed by Malachi Bartlett, as were all Witney Railway stations. The offices were on the Up platform, which was the station's only platform until wartime exigencies required a passing loop, which resulted in the Down platform being opened on 6 August 1944. The station had always been busy, in the 1920s dealing with 12,000 tons of freight and booking 14,000 passenger tickets. It closed to goods on 26 April 1965.

Eynsham station was the scene of violence in 1927. On 26 September an Essex policeman stopped two men driving a stolen car and was shot dead by one of the criminals. Still at liberty, the murderer, Frederick Browne, who had once lived in Eynsham, decided to raid the station safe. Wearing masks and armed with revolvers, the pair drove to South Leigh and bumped over the sleepers to Eynsham station. The porter there, Frederick Castle, was ordered to put his hands up and marched to the stationmaster's office, the door of which had been forced. Later he was taken to the west end of the yard and trussed up in the ground frame cabin. From the station the thieves stole several parcels and a typewriter. Browne was arrested in London on 20 January 1928, found guilty and executed on 31 May of that year.

South Leigh station was similar in architectural style to that at Eynsham, but was built on a smaller scale. At the far end of the goods loop siding a Ministry of Food cold store opened during the Second World War. About 1¾ miles beyond the station was Ballaso Bridge, the name being a corruption of 'ballast hole', this feature being situated in a copse south of the line.

At Witney goods junction the original Witney Railway curved north-west to the goods yard, passenger trains continuing west on the EGR to the passenger station. Like all EGR stations, this one had a single storey and was constructed of Cotswold stone. At some time a large canopy was added to it. Water cranes were provided on both platforms. The EGR stations were all on the same general plan. Moving from west to east the rooms were: parcels office, office accommodation, general waiting room, ladies' waiting room and toilets.

In the goods yard there was a large Cotswold stone goods shed, which at various times extended at both ends, while the original timber passenger station was also used for goods purposes. The engine shed closed in January 1873. There were stables for the railway horses and in due course these were converted to a road motor depot. The yard had seven sidings, which were kept busy with coal, blankets, agricultural produce and cattle. Blankets were pressure packed in standard bales. Harrods used to have one train load annually. The blanket traffic was lost to the road in 1966. In about 1935 the yard handled about 50,000 tons of freight annually. By 1957 this had changed to 44,000 tons of goods and 66,000 parcels. Goods traffic brought in £70,000 in the last year of operation.

Immediately beyond the passenger station was the first of the EGR overbridges. Looking extremely narrow, they had a single wooden parapet, which in some cases was replaced by corrugated iron.

Bampton, renamed Bampton (Oxon) on 2 July 1906 and Brize Norton & Bampton (Oxon) on 1 May 1940, had a station building similar to that at Witney. The village of Bampton was 1¾ miles distant. On 22 October 1936, beyond the station and goods yard, a private siding left the branch to assist construction of the RAF runway, but, following the opening of the airfield in August 1937, it closed in 1938.

Carterton station was only 1¼ miles beyond Bampton. The village of Carterton was built by William Carter, who bought a large acreage and developed it as smallholdings. The two-road station opened on 2 October 1944 to serve RAF stations at Brize Norton, Broadwell and the Women's Land Army hostel at Shilton. Traffic despatched included day-old chicks, mushrooms and tame mice. The station building was a typical War Department structure, with an asbestos canopy sheltering the platform.

Alvescot, ¾ mile further on, had a single platform. This EGR station was constructed of red brick. It had no signal-box, the siding being controlled from ground frames. In 1947 the line here was blocked by a huge snowdrift, but trains were run to either side and passengers crossed on foot between them.

Kelmscott & Langford station also had a single platform. Opened on 4 November 1907, the station building was formed from two standard GWR pagodas of the type used for halts, but this was in fact a station, even though it was staffed by just one man. A siding, worked from a ground frame, was added on 9 July 1928 for loading and unloading cattle and farm machinery. Before reaching Lechlade station the line crossed into Gloucestershire.

A 517 class 0–4–2T hauled the opening train on the EGR. 'Metro' class 2–4–0T No. 3588 started working the branch in 1899, and this class worked the line for fifty years until the last was withdrawn in December 1949. 1854 class 0–6–0STs and 'Dean Goods' were used on freight trains. The last of the 'Queen' class 2–2–2 engines saw out their twilight years, and No. 1128, the final survivor, succumbed in April 1914. No. 165, the last GWR 2–2–2, worked the branch until its withdrawal in December 1914. Both No. 165 and No. 1128 were fitted with ATC apparatus.

In the 1950s, 0–6–0PTs of the 57XX and 74XX classes handled most of the branch traffic, but 45XX and 55XX 2–6–2Ts and 14XX 0–4–2Ts also appeared. Latterly, 2251 class 0–6–0s were common. Some off-peak services were operated by GWR diesel railcars. The last steam engine working on the branch, by now freight only, was a 2–6–2T on 31 December 1965. Monday 3 January 1966 saw a Class 22 Bo-Bo diesel-hydraulic at work. 'Foreign' engines on the line were extremely rare, but an LNER class B12 4–6–0 worked an ambulance train to Fairford in 1944.

The Witney Railway opened with four trains each way, this frequency remaining when the line was extended to Fairford. No trains ran on Sundays. By 1910 the service had increased to five each way and an Oxford to Witney return trip, plus one to Fairford and back on Sundays. In 1938, five trains still ran the whole length of the branch, but the number of intermediate services had increased: two Oxford to Bampton and back and two Oxford to Witney and back. On Sundays, in addition to the return train to Fairford, one ran from Oxford to Bampton and back. Almost without exception, trains called at all stations. In 1911, passenger trains consisted of: one guard's van, one first, two third, two composite and one brake-third, all of which were six-wheel stock.

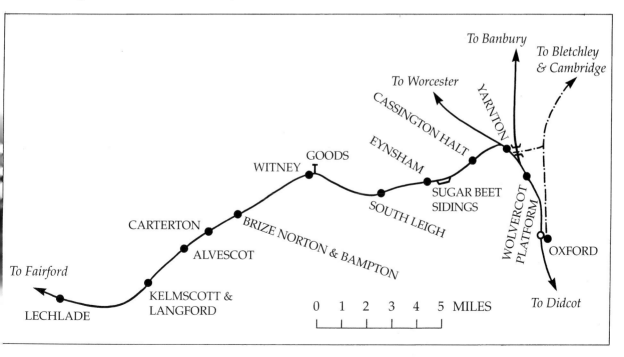

A 74XX class 0–6–0PT, No. 7412, at Oxford motive power depot. This engine worked on the Witney branch.

18.5.61 Revd Alan Newman

Yarnton Junction, view Up. Notice the unusual waiting shelter with the curious supports to its corrugated iron roof.

c. 1960 Lens of Sutton

Yarnton Junction, view Down. The Witney branch curves left.

c. 1960 Lens of Sutton

Cassington Halt with a concrete platform.

c. 1960 Lens of Sutton

A ganger's tricycle, which was used for track inspection, near Cassington Halt. A hammer and spanner are clipped to the outrigger.

c. 1930 Author's collection

The single platform at Eynsham station. Notice the well-tended garden in the foreground.

c. 1910 Lens of Sutton

An 8750 class 0–6–0PT, No. 9640, at the new Down platform, Eynsham station.

9.7.59 Author's collection

South Leigh station, view Up.

c. 1948 J.H. Russell

Extensions have been made at both ends of the goods shed, Witney station. Notice that the van is in GWR livery and that the mechanical horse trailer is in BR livery.

c. 1948 J.H. Russell

A four-coach Down train at Witney, hauled by a 'Metro' class 2–4–0T. Notice the tracks converging before the ends of the platforms. This is because they have to meet before the single line passes under a narrow bridge. The message on the reverse of the postcard reads: 'Dear Old Barn. This is the station we take the milk to. The train has just come from Oxford and I don't know where it is bound for. Write soon. Lots of love. Belle.' The card is postmarked 13.9.20.

c. 1910 Paul Strong collection

Witney, view Down. The engine on the Up train could be a 2–2–2. Notice the non-slip, brick-surfaced platform, and the clerestory coach (left). Flower beds embellish the station.

c. 1910 Lens of Sutton

Brize Norton & Bampton station was known as Bampton (Oxon) station until 1 May 1940. A crowd awaits an Up train. The platform appears to have been lengthened at some time.

c. 1920 Lens of Sutton

The Down platform of Brize Norton & Bampton station from the 12.18 p.m. Oxford to Fairford service.

2.7.60 Author

Carterton opened on 2 October 1944. This Up view shows the rather austere construction of the canopy. Notice the unusually narrow appearance of the standard EGR overbridge.

c. 1960 Lens of Sutton

A 74XX class 0–6–0PT, No. 7404, about to depart from Carterton with the 4.38 p.m. Carterton to Oxford service. This train did not run through to the terminus at Fairford.

2.6.54 Hugh Ballantyne

Alvescot, view Down. Notice the corrugated iron goods shed in front of the passenger station, the yard weighbridge and hut (left); and the pile of tree trunks at the far end of the goods yard.

c. 1955 Lens of Sutton

Kelmscott & Langford station opened on 4 November 1908. These workmen have probably been putting the finishing touches to the halt. The earth platform is held behind a brick wall. This is unusual as halts of this period were often of timber construction.

c. 1908 Lens of Sutton

A 74XX class 0–6–0PT, No. 7412, at Kelmscott & Langford station with an Up train.

5.7.58 E. Wilmshurst